A Professional's Guide to Decision Science and Problem Solving

A Professional's Guide to Decision Science and Problem Solving

An Integrated Approach for Assessing Issues, Finding Solutions, and Reaching Corporate Objectives

Frank A. Tillman
Deandra T. Cassone

Vice President, Publisher: Tim Moore
Associate Publisher and Director of Marketing: Amy Neidlinger
Executive Editor: Jeanne Glasser Levine
Editorial Assistant: Pamela Boland
Development Editor: Russ Hall
Operations Manager: Jodi Kemper
Senior Marketing Manager: Julie Phifer
Assistant Marketing Manager: Megan Graue
Cover Designer: Alan Clements
Managing Editor: Kristy Hart
Project Editor: Jovana San Nicolas-Shirley
Copy Editor: Apostrophe Editing Services
Proofreader: Williams Woods Publishing Services
Indexer: Erika Millen
Compositor: Nonie Ratcliff
Manufacturing Buyer: Dan Uhrig

© 2012 by Frank A. Tillman and Deandra T. Cassone
Publishing as FT Press
Upper Saddle River, New Jersey 07458

FT Press offers excellent discounts on this book when ordered in quantity for bulk purchases or special sales. For more information, please contact U.S. Corporate and Government Sales, 1-800-382-3419, corpsales@pearsontechgroup.com. For sales outside the U.S., please contact International Sales at international@pearson.com.

Company and product names mentioned herein are the trademarks or registered trademarks of their respective owners.

Printed in the United States of America

First Printing March 2012

ISBN-10: 0-13-286978-0
ISBN-13: 978-0-13-286978-2

Pearson Education LTD.
Pearson Education Australia PTY, Limited.
Pearson Education Singapore, Pte. Ltd.
Pearson Education Asia, Ltd.
Pearson Education Canada, Ltd.
Pearson Educación de Mexico, S.A. de C.V.
Pearson Education—Japan
Pearson Education Malaysia, Pte. Ltd.

The Library of Congress cataloging-in-publishing data is on file.

We would like to dedicate this book to Dr. C. L. Hwang. Through the course of his academic career, Dr. Hwang researched and assessed an exhaustive list of Multiple Attribute, Multiple Objective, and Group Decision-Making techniques in both the crisp and fuzzy environments, which are published in six of his books. Dr. Hwang was an early pioneer in the field of Decision Science and his contributions to this field are still realized today in academia and at the heart of this book. He introduced this area of study to the authors who worked together with him for a number of years.

Contents

Acknowledgments

We would like to thank our family members who have continually supported us in the development of this book. Barbara Tillman (my mother) has spent countless hours listening to my father (Frank A. Tillman, Ph.D.— author) and me talk about our ideas and the content of this book. She has always been our greatest supporter. We'd like to thank all our family members who have endured our discussions about this book at our family events. The family members include my sister, Michelle Hoyt, and her son, Alan Tillman, my sister and brother-in-law, Lisa Lacey, D.O. and Ron Lacey, M.D., and their two children, Ben and Nic Lacey, and my three children, Kasey, Kristina, and Victor Cassone who have all been extremely supportive in this effort.

Additionally, we would like to thank Abhik Barua and Paul Sapenaro for their review of the content of this book. With Abhik's background and experience, he provided suggestions in the presentation and content of the material. Paul's experience as a Fortune 100 executive and his expertise in the field of leadership and project management provided insights into the application of project management concepts in the business process execution. Both Abhik and Paul are great thinkers and provided insights to help mold this book into the final product.

We would also like to thank Jeanne Glasser Levine for her belief and support of this effort. Jeanne was exceptional in her ability to see our vision for the book and position it within the industry. Her knowledge of the industry and insight into the value of material was a driving force in publishing this book.

Also, we would like to acknowledge C.L. Hwang, Ph.D., and his lifelong contribution to the field of Decision Science. The combination of his research and Dr. Tillman's research and the application of many practical Decision Science methods in consulting is an important contribution to the methods applied and discussed within the framework of this book.

—Frank A. Tillman, Ph.D. and Deandra Tillman Cassone, Ph.D.

About the Authors

Frank A. Tillman has had a varied and full career teaching and doing research in academia for more than 30 years, starting and managing two consulting firms, IBES, Inc. (government agencies) and HTX International, Inc. (private firms), and developing commercial and residential real estate. He served as department head at Kansas State University for more than 20 years where he published 50+ professional articles, published two books, and advised a number of M.S. and Ph.D. theses candidates. This book is a compilation of his consulting experiences noting which approach works best to solve real problems that result in solutions that can be implemented.

Deandra T. Cassone currently teaches as an adjunct professor at Missouri University of Science and Technology in its graduate systems engineering program and is in management at a Fortune 100 company. She has spent more than 25 year in the industry, serving in consulting, technical, and management roles. Her interests lie in building structured decision-making models that encompass the application of the concepts in this book. She has also submitted and been awarded a number of business process patents.

Preface

Executives must know how well their company operates compared to others in the industry. By looking at industry benchmarks, you can learn where companies excel and where improvement is needed. The approach in this book can help you pinpoint specific areas that show the most promise for improvement and how they can ultimately impact upstream and downstream functions. It is vital that lower-level decisions support the overall corporate goals. You can evaluate the product line in regard to which product should be put into the product line and which should be dropped. You can access the supply chain to determine areas in which performance improvements should be focused. You can weight mergers for their impact on current operations and whether the merger is the right move. This book presents a unique approach for the first time and the included case studies provide insights into how you can apply the steps of the approach.

This book integrates new and existing methods to provide a comprehensive and holistic approach for assessing company performance and identifying areas for corporate improvement efforts. Many times, you look at the problem in a stove pipe manner and try to solve what appear to be key issues from a singular perspective. You must take a global, holistic approach to understand the overall impact a problem has on the entire organization. All organizations have multiple interactions, so you must look at the upstream interactions and the impact on the downstream functions before any decisions are made.

This process is geared toward all levels of an organization. The goal is to get people to think of the big picture and understand the tools and techniques that they can use to solve corporate-wide problems. The difficulty is to know when and where you should use these concepts. Understanding the problem and the environment, and analyzing the information and quantifying results involve putting the conceptual and analytical pieces together to solve the presented problem. You can use this basic process from the production floor to the board room. It is based on applying the right solution approach to the problem and generating a sound, implementable solution.

In general, corporate planning approaches are based on establishing a vision, doing a situation analysis, setting objectives, and developing strategies. This new approach incorporates some of these characteristics; however, it focuses on structured analysis processes that you can use to quantify, explore, and solve problems from a cross-functional perspective. Depending on the executive, a traditional strategic planning approach may be conducted by a vice president for a given functional area. The traditional approach would focus on optimizing this particular area. It is crucial, however, to ensure that the optimization of one functional area does not negatively impact another. This is why the integrated, cross-functional approach to problem solving is critical to benefit the company as a whole.

If organizations approach problem solving from a corporate perspective, the organization will undoubtedly become an effective and more efficient operation. The solution then is based on an overall objective approach, and not on individual agendas, and a well-operating environment such as this is a true measure of the future success of a company.

The breadth of problems that this approach can address is large, including new product development, inventory level optimization, logistics modeling, manpower planning, budget allocation, and many other applications. *Knowing where to begin, what to assess, how to look for workable solutions, and what to measure provides effective solutions that can be implemented by the entire organization and is the key objective of this book.*

It is easy to get mired into details, overlook key elements of the problem, and not know what techniques are most appropriate. Time is always of the essence, so solutions must be quickly developed to solve problems in an ever changing environment.

Experienced employees are important to any organization. The knowledge they possess provides valuable insight into the operation of the organization. Individuals with different educational backgrounds and experiences have a variety of ideas and perspectives in how the organization should operate. Experience must be part of the decision process along with the available data to make sound business decisions. Different opinions can lead to a wide variety of approaches in solving problems and accomplishing the company's strategic goals.

Quantifiable measures, however, should be used to support and justify decisions whenever available.

Data can show the condition of the organization and the efficiency of the operating environment. Making decisions without supporting facts and information can lead to less than optimal decisions that may not be justified when looking at the company's bottom line. It is critical to support experience, expert opinion, and judgment with factual data. It is much easier to justify a course of action with "the data shows" instead of "I think or believe." Unfounded opinions can more easily be dispelled with facts rather than succumbing to the power of strong-willed individuals arguing for their solution.

This book presents an upper-level management perspective of how to analyze problems. The intent is to show what information is needed, the approach, and useful methods that you should use. Observing the problem and its political environment is equally as important as knowing how to analyze the problem and arrive at a sound, acceptable solution.

A clear understanding of organizational objectives provides direction and focus for the corporation. Typically, there are many different areas of opportunity to pursue with limited resources. A clear picture and evaluation of the organization environment and the interaction between functions provides a framework to understand and evaluate the issues facing the corporation. Sound assessment of the issues within the company is critical to pinpointing key issues and opportunity areas. Measuring these key issues provides an understanding of the progress and success in improvement efforts.

Steps and methods are presented in this book to walk you through the process to identify corporate issues and develop solutions that can direct the corporation to achieve its goals. The structured thought process and solid evaluation of corporate functions and issues used in this book can drive a corporation to improvement as measured by key performance metrics. This provides a roadmap to identify the key areas in which improvements are required that can best impact the bottom line. The following sections of the book explain this process, and case studies are presented in the last three chapters of the book. The first case study describes how you can apply this integrated process to supply chain management. The second case study addresses the assessment and decision making surrounding new product development decisions. The last case study addresses key areas that should be assessed and analyzed in a corporate merger. The goal is for you to not only read the book, but also to apply these concepts to your own organization.

Following is a summary of the chapters:

- **Chapter 1, "Define the Objectives and Identify Metrics"**— You need to clearly articulate and document the objectives of a corporation. Each of the multiple functions within a company has different objectives with varying importance, and many of the high-level objectives of the corporation may conflict. It is vital for senior management to articulate these objectives and reach an overall consensus of the weighted importance so that these objectives can be included into the corporate decision process at all levels.

- **Chapter 2, "Explore the Environment"**—This chapter presents a new approach to integrated corporate planning. Assessments are made with key corporate functions to determine the closeness or dependence of the functional relationships that you can use as a guide to identify the scope of functional areas for improvement. Additionally, benchmarking, variability analysis, and budget contributions are assessed to expand beyond the relationships to evaluate how well these functions perform against industry competitors.

- **Chapter 3, "Explore the Scope of the Problem and Its Importance"**—Critical in this analysis is not only identifying the corporate issues, but also determining the upstream and downstream process and operational impact associated with improving these processes. High-level business process modeling is discussed. Often fixing one problem can cause an issue in another area, and this step ensures that you address the various operational impacts in the analysis.

- **Chapter 4, "Data Mining and Statistical Analysis"**—This chapter highlights the importance of data analysis. Recognizing the problems and determining where improvements should be made is critical. Understanding the information that can quantify and support improvements provides a factual basis for justifying changes to operations and processes. This chapter presents a number of methods to analyze data with further detail of the methods provided in the appendices.

- **Chapter 5, "Solve the Problem and Measure the Results"**—After the analysis is performed, as shown in Chapters 1 through 4, the approach to solving the problem is developed. Often, assessing the environment and performing the data analysis can lead to a clear solution. In other cases, you might require computer-based solutions or more sophisticated methods. *The best solution is one that the decision maker understands and uses.* This chapter focuses on determining the best methods that the data and environment can support.

- **Chapter 6, "Evaluate the Results and Do Sensitivity Analysis"**—This chapter discusses how to use the decision model to explore the results and determine their economic viability. A well-defined model has the functional capability to change key parameters and constraints and determine the impact of those changes on the final solution. "What-if" analysis is a key ingredient in the decision process. The sensitivity of the variables in the solution must be tested to ensure that the best solution is reached.

- **Chapter 7, "Summary of Part I"**—This chapter brings together the approach and highlights the key points from the analyses.

- **Chapter 8, "Logistics Service Provider"**—This chapter applies the process described in this book to a full-service supply chain provider. The step-by-step analysis is performed to show how to implement this approach in the logistics environment.

- **Chapter 9, "New Product Development"**—This chapter applies the process to a company with its core competencies and how new products can be developed. A structured approach to decision making is developed based on the interrelationships and performance of the company.

- **Chapter 10, "Airline Merger"**—This chapter addresses some of the key considerations to analyze and assess when merging two companies. Performance and functional interactions of the companies are assessed, which is key to evaluating the activities for the airlines.

- **Appendix A, "Overview of Methodologies"**—This appendix provides a high-level overview of various analytical and decision science methodologies which can be used to evaluate and formulate problem solutions.

- **Appendix B, "Detailed Methodologies"**—This appendix provides the mathematical background for methods that are useful in model development.

Part I

The Method

1

Define the Objectives
and Identify Metrics

1.1 Chapter Topic

This chapter discusses the importance of clearly articulating and documenting the objectives of a corporation. Each of the multiple functions within a company has different objectives with differing importance. Many of the high-level objectives of the corporation may be conflicting. Senior management must articulate these objectives and reach an overall consensus of the weight of importance of these objectives if the corporation is to improve and measure the success of meeting them. This chapter also discusses the development of decision criteria and metrics. This involves defining specific quantifiable measures to determine whether the objectives are met. You need to capture the weights or importance of these decision criteria and metrics to appropriately measure improvement.

1.2 Key Corporate Participants

Senior executives identify the problem and establish the task force to work on the problem with an executive-level cross-functional team of representatives. Executive management articulates the corporate objectives and communicates these objectives to the organization so that it can form a workforce team for the cross-functional problem solving. The executive-level task force representatives then update the management by progress reports and findings.

1.3 Management Steps Required to Execute the Approach

You need to follow some basic steps to solve difficult cross-functional problems, as shown in Figure 1.1. Throughout this book, you can see the details surrounding this approach. You need to establish upfront that this approach requires executive-level commitment and buy-in to be successful. A primary goal of the process is to drive the corporate objectives into a cross-functional analysis that best solves problems for the company as a whole. To accomplish this, senior executives must establish or communicate the objectives and support the overall approach so that the appropriate executives, managers, and subject matter experts also engage in the process.

Next to each of the steps listed in Figure 1.1, you can identify the management level required for the process. Each level of management serves an important part in the process. The executive levels of vice president and director must be committed to contribute so that the issues important to their organization and the interactions between the cross-functional organizations are represented in the process. Managers and subject matter experts conduct the actual analyses and assessments based on the overall organizational goals. When gathering the data used in the analysis, it requires involving those that gather and use this data at each level of the organization. Each layer of management and individual contributors play a part in driving corporate objectives into the solutions developed at each level through this process.

A project manager (with a Project Management Professional [PMP] certification) or an internal project manager should coordinate the effort. This project manager can coordinate the meetings with the task force and core team; establish time lines; ensure that the activity remains within scope, schedule, and cost; and provide status updates to executives. Additionally, the project manager must facilitate the definition of functional and system requirements and provide those requirements to the appropriate executing organization, such as IT or various operational groups. Project management techniques provide an excellent way to coordinate an activity such as this.

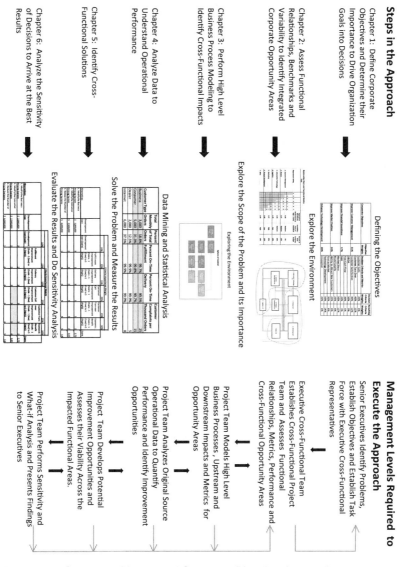

Figure 1.1 Overview of Integrated Corporate Planning Approach

Identifying the goals and objectives of the organization requires upper management involvement in setting goals and communicating these goals to the decision makers at all levels of the organization. Upper management is interviewed by facilitators who utilize Group Decision-Making techniques to help determine a consensus of the corporate objectives. This involves discussing the corporate and departmental objectives and goals with all the business components, such as operations, sales, marketing, and finance.

To understand the problem, you must understand the decisions that must be made at each level. This includes defining the questions so that the answers are consistent with the corporate and individual goals. The answers to the following questions should support overall corporate goals.

- How much should I produce of a product in each of the product lines?
- What research items should be funded?
- What are my warehousing requirements?
- How does my production affect my inventory requirements?
- What should I plan to produce to meet customer demand?
- How can I optimize scheduling delivery vehicles?
- And, many others.

You must also determine what you can actually change and what you cannot change within the organization. For example, if an organization wants to determine products to keep in a product line, it is not likely that the flagship items should be removed from the product line without considering their impact on all products.

Fixed operating constraints that you cannot change may also exist. This may include any number of constraints on current operations such as plant capacities, warehouse space, and the amount of resources available for spending in a given year. Usually a whole range of operating constraints exists from manufacturing, warehousing, distribution, and other areas of the company that affect the decision latitude that can be made.

You need to define the operating constraints and the variables associated with the actual decisions to be made, such as things that can be rationally changed in the normal course of business operations. This may include things such as plant throughput, funding of programs, sales commission structures, and others. The idea here is to determine what decisions can be made or changed and what cannot be changed. Understanding the decision limitations within an organization defines the operating constraints of the decision process.

This part of the process involves determining the best criteria or means to measure the success of meeting the objectives and goals in the model. These criteria with their measures or metrics provide the decision maker with a quantification of the degree of success in achieving the goals of the organization. Based on the goals and objectives established previously, this part of the process involves determining the data sources and potential data elements that you can use as measures of success for the organization. You can gather these metrics from organizational data sources or from experts within the organization. First identifying those criteria that specifically measure the objectives is a key step before determining if data is available for the associated metric. Sometimes, a good metric may not have data that you can easily obtain to support it.

Maintaining metrics can be cumbersome. Keeping the number of criteria small, say around 5, should be sufficient. Decisions are usually made on only one or two key criteria, and the rest don't actually influence the decision. Perform sensitivity analysis to determine which of the metrics are the key metrics.

The result of this are the definition of the objectives and then the decisions to be made and the metrics used to measure the success of the proposed decisions.

1.4 Solving the Right Problem

The process of organizational decision making is complex because executives have their own goals independent of the corporate goals. The challenge is to balance the individual objectives and goals with the corporate objectives and goals both in the short and long term.

Traditionally, decisions are made in a stovepipe fashion. That is, each functional area makes decisions that are best for it without regard to the needs of the other functions; for example, manufacturing is not concerned with marketing or distribution or finance. The reason for this is the reward system for each functional area focuses only on the efficiency for that system. That is, the plant manager or operations manager is rewarded for such things as utilization of assets, return on assets, throughput, quality, minimum labor cost, and scrap for the units produced. None of these factors measure marketing efficiencies or any other functions. Marketing, for example, is basically measured and rewarded for total sales and not on specific products or product mix. When each function goes its separate way and decisions are made that improve that single function, who is looking out for the company as a whole? It begs the question, "Who is running the company?" Is it running by default where the strongest personality drives the company from their functional perspective? How, then, can you develop an overall plan for the good of the company where individual functions are sacrificed a little for the overall good? This may result in manufacturing making products that don't fully utilize the production assets; where marketing doesn't maximize the total volume sales but sells an optimum mix of products that maximize customer service and maximize profitability. You can then see it would be much better overall if there were a combined reward system so that the overall good of the organization is achieved in place of individual goals in the short and long term.

This leads to the issue of how best to manage the many objectives and how to trade off between them so that the entire organization prospers now and in the future. To do this you must first state the organization's goals and objectives. You must first specifically determine what these goals are in the short term and for the future and then set up metrics to measure how well you accomplish them. One way to do this is to ask some difficult questions. What are you trying to accomplish within the company? What are you trying to accomplish at each organizational level? Unfortunately, most firms do not spend time asking these questions, or if they do, they don't implement the answers into their everyday operations. Why does this happen in nearly all the corporations, large and small and at every level? Although everyone's intentions are good in setting corporate objectives, the major problem is that with today's approach to management, the objectives are ill-defined and consequently impossible to implement. How then can you ensure the corporate objectives are implemented throughout the organization, and how can you measure their success? The primary reason corporate objectives are not implemented at the operations level (which is the only place they can make an impact) is that they usually are subservient to individual managers' objectives.

Thus you must ask, "How can we get there if we don't know where we are going?" More specifically, what are you trying to accomplish at the corporate level, at the functional level, and most important at the individual or action level? A great deal of effort goes into establishing a 3-year plan and identifying a number of corporate objectives with everyone pretending to agree, knowing full well the plan will be put on the shelf and promptly forgotten after the exercise is over.

1.5 Developing an Understanding of the Problem

This phase of the process is focused on developing an understanding of what the organization wants to accomplish. In this process you ask the difficult questions and correctly interpret the answers that reveal the correct problems.

Answering these questions requires getting key individuals to look closely at what they each want to accomplish individually and companywide. This process takes thought and reflection by management. Starting this type of thought process makes management focus on its individual needs and then integrate them into the overall needs of the organization. Many times, individuals are not overtly aware of how solving their problems impacts the other divisions within their company. Bringing these individuals together and addressing the problems forces them to look at their problems as total organizational problems.

1.6 Defining Goals and Objectives of a Company or Organization

You can use a number of different methods and approaches to define corporate goals and objectives, using formal and informal procedures. Doing this can provide the organization with a definition of its goals and objectives that represent its current thinking. These goals and objectives can then be integrated into the decision-making process so that decisions made with the decision model are structured to impact all levels of the organization and are quantifiable and defensible.

In establishing corporate goals and objectives, consider using management to get a group consensus. Available group decision-making techniques vary in degrees of formality and you can use them to facilitate this process. Techniques range from simple brainstorming to more sophisticated methods. The end result should be a clear definition of what a corporation views as its goals and objectives. When defined, these goals and objectives can then be built into the decision process. Following is a sequence of steps that you can use to establish the goals and objectives of an organization.

1.6.1 Establish Goals and Objectives

The first step involves establishing the objectives for the organization. Primary decision makers should meet together to ensure that all the components of the organization are represented in the decision process and are represented in the objectives. One approach is to provide to the group a "straw man" list of corporate objectives as a starting point in the development of the final list of objectives. The straw man list is based on the objectives that have historically been deemed important to the group and may include objectives such as maximizing profitability, minimizing risk, minimizing cost, or maximizing growth. The executive group can then use these as a starting point and brainstorm to add or delete from the list. As part of this process, the group should also provide a high-level definition of the objectives so that all involved understand what is meant by them.

Another method, the Nominal Group Technique (NGT), which utilizes a written form for the generation of ideas, is a more formalized method that you can use to develop corporate objectives. This method attempts to minimize conforming influences and maintain social-emotional relationships in the process. It provides for equality of participation and for all members to influence the group decision through voting and ordering of priorities. Appendix A, "Overview of Methodologies," provides a description of this method, along with several others that can be used in this process.

Managers may not have the authority to affect high-level decisions; however, the establishment of these objectives and the development of the subsequent decision criteria and metrics give managers a defensible position in their decisions. The objectives established in this manner can provide the building blocks for establishing the decision criteria and metrics used within the decision model.

It is also beneficial to establish a mission statement for the organization. A mission statement is a succinct statement, typically one sentence that summarizes the purpose of the organization. A mission statement describes why the organization is in business and what it wants to accomplish.

When any group of individuals meets to conduct activities such as this, it is difficult to arrive at complete agreement. You need to understand upfront that this may be the case. In this process, you must leave the latitude to "agree to disagree." That is, it is okay if there is not complete agreement on all the objectives. Not all objectives may have the same importance to each function of an organization. Weighting the objectives, as described in the next section, provides a means to address that not all individuals may feel the same about the importance of each objective, which can be handled in the modeling process.

Examples of corporate objectives by different industries are shown here.

- Service companies
  - Improve contract performance.
  - Minimize operating costs.
  - Improve customer management.

- Manufacturing companies
  - Minimize manufacturing costs.
  - Maximize customer service.
  - Minimize distribution costs.

- Distribution companies
  - Minimize operating costs.
  - Reduce inventory levels.
  - Improve operating cycle time.

- Insurance companies
  - Maximize customer service.
  - Streamline information technology.
  - Improve service delivery margin.
- Food Industry companies
  - Improve profitability.
  - Increase market share.
  - Increase sales.
  - Reduce manufacturing costs.
  - Reduce distribution costs.

These objectives are broad in nature and can focus management on organizational-level goals. Objectives are weighted to further focus corporate management on key operating areas within the company. Specific decision criteria and metrics further refine the key attributes that constitute the corporate measurement of the objectives. The objectives provide the starting point for the decomposition of strategic goals into actionable activities and problem solving.

1.6.1.1 Expert Judgment/Group Participation

The problem of group decision making can be broadly classified into two categories in this field: expert judgment and group consensus. The expert judgment process entails making a decision by using expertise gained through experience. Specifically, it is concerned with making judgments and constructing new solutions to the problem. On the other hand, the group consensus process involves groups that have common interests, such as executive boards and organizations, making a decision.

Expert judgment and group consensus methods involve methods commonly utilized in the group decision-making process. Creative methods used to extract, generate, and stimulate new ideas may include brainstorming, brainwriting, or Nominal Group technique. Techniques that are used to explore and clarify existing issues might include surveys, conferences, and the Successive Proportional

Additive Numeration (SPAN) technique. For planning and execution, you can use techniques such as Gantt charts, PERT, and CPM. (Refer to Appendix B, "Detailed Methodologies," for a detailed description of methods.)

1.6.1.2 Weight the Objectives to Determine Their Importance

Many times goals and objectives can be stated as being important to an organization but the relative importance of them is not quantified. In addition, there are typically conflicting objectives in which the improvement in one area may adversely impact another area. For example, improvements in information technology may also lead to increases in capital costs. This step is to generate an overall importance for each of the established goals and objectives. This is accomplished by having each of the team members weigh the objectives established in the previous step for their view of overall importance in decisions. You can use the Normalized Direct Weighting scheme described next to weigh the objectives. You can also use a more complex weighing scheme such as SPAN or Borda, but they require automation to be practical. (Refer to Appendix B for a detailed description of methods.)

A weighting scheme for the example objectives of Maximize Customer Satisfaction, Minimize Logistics Costs, Maximize Growth, and Maximize Sales is shown in Table 1.1. This weighting scheme was generated by the Normalized Direct Weighting scheme. A set of weights should be generated by each of the team members. These can then be averaged to determine a group weighting of the objectives. In this example, each of the four individuals weighted the objectives on a scale of 1 to 10, where 10 was the most important. These then are totaled and normalized for the individuals and the group overall.

Objective weighting can come from senior management's view of corporate strategic direction. Another approach to weighting objectives is to determine the percent of budget that falls within a given corporate functional area. Weighting objectives using the number of dollars quantifies the magnitude of financial importance associated with a functional area. This provides a view of the potential impacts of improvement opportunities for a given functional area.

Table 1.1 Group Consensus Weighting of Objectives

OBJECTIVE	Expert #1 Input	Expert #1 Weights	Expert #2 Input	Expert #2 Weights	Expert #3 Input	Expert #3 Weights	Expert #4 Input	Expert #4 Weights	Total Input Values	Overall Weight
Maximize Customer Satisfaction	9	28.10%	10	30.30%	10	33.30%	9	30.00%	38	30.40%
Minimize Logistics Costs	6	18.80%	7	21.20%	3	10.00%	4	13.30%	20	16.00%
Maximize Growth	9	28.10%	7	21.20%	7	23.30%	9	30.00%	32	25.60%
Maximize Sales	8	25.00%	9	27.30%	10	33.30%	8	26.70%	35	28.00%
TOTAL	32		33		30		30		125	

Assigning an overall importance weighting to the objectives gives the decision makers an idea of what the group as a whole views as the importance of the objectives for the organization. These objectives and their importance also provide the necessary direction and focus in the decision modeling process. You now have a better idea of what you can accomplish as an organization.

1.7 Defining the Framework for the Decisions Being Made

You need to know what the organization wants to accomplish, the purpose of the decisions being made, and the operating environment of the organization. You can then develop the decision model to reflect the conditions and characteristics of the organization. Use the following questions to aid in defining the framework for the model.

- What specific decisions need to be made?
- What are the business environment and constraints in which decisions are made?
- What are the firm constraints within which to achieve the goals and objectives?
- What is the flexibility of the decision to be made to achieve the goals?

Use various fact-finding efforts to answer these questions. Depending on the breadth of the model, this may require that you conduct interviews with individuals in various departments and levels within the organization. Individuals currently responsible for the decisions and individuals that have been previously responsible for the decisions are good starting points to gain information. At this point in the development, this should still only be general information that you can use to outline the model being developed.

Decisions to be made with the model would dictate the structure of the model. Some examples of decisions might include the following:

- Establish budgets for the divisions and corporation as a whole.
- Determine which products should be in the product line.
- List the warehouse requirements.

- Compile the least-cost production scheduling options.
- Assess the facility conditions.
- Examine the personnel management and number and skill mix of employees.

Part of answering these questions and the nature of the information gathered in the modeling process may provide additional information that you can use to make decisions. For example, use a decision model to allocate resources. However, this can also provide an opportunity to standardize the submission format of budget requests and potentially do various database queries on the submitted budget data to determine how well you make the budget.

The business environment in which the decisions are made is also important in the decision process. In an organizational environment that is dictatorial, no matter what the justification for the decision, the model may be of no use. If it is a group consensus organization, the model should reflect that type of decision-making process so that it is representative of the organization. The model should be focused forward and adaptable to changes. For example, if a division combines with another division in the next 3 months, this should be accounted for in the model structure. These types of events should be investigated in the model development process.

To determine the framework for the model, you need to identify what elements of the operating environment are fixed and what elements of the environment can change. Fixed constraints would include those elements that have permanent limitations or restrictions in the decision process. In a production environment, it could be limitations on quantities that can be produced, steps in the manufacturing process required to create an item, warehouse limitations, and others. In budget decisions, this could involve the resource limits, limits on certain types of projects or programs funded, and others. In manpower planning, there may be limitations on the mix of skills required to perform certain activities or restrictions based on union requirements. A general overall understanding of what cannot change is as important as understanding what can be changed in the model.

Understanding the decision variables that represent the decisions to be made by the organization is equally important. Again, these variables are dependent upon the business environment of an organization and impact the type of model being built. With a model in a production environment, variables might include the amount of safety stock that is kept in-house or at remote locations or quantities of various products produced. With a model used for resource allocation, the decision may be which research and development projects you should fund.

The accuracy of the model is also an important consideration in the model development process. If a model must be accurate to a high level, such as 99 percent, the level of detail required will be much greater than for a model that must be accurate to 95 percent or 90 percent. The type of data and information processing will be different for these two modeling scenarios.

Overall, Group Decision-Making techniques can be useful in many consensus-building situations within the organizational environment. These techniques are used (as shown in the next chapter) to facilitate the establishment of corporate goals and objectives and in building decision models. Your goal here is to determine what is important to the organization and what is your future direction.

1.8 Metrics for Measuring Success

When an organization has defined and agreed upon its goals and objectives, decision makers should then develop a means to track and measure the accomplishment of these objectives. Often within an organization, a strategic plan, short-range plan, or long-range plan is developed and published as an edict to the organization. These plans may, however, end up on a shelf with no real meaning in the day-to-day operation of the organization. To drive these goals into the operating decision levels within the organization, these goals and objectives must be translated to meaningful measures of success that are used within the decision process and tracked within the organization. This is key to ensuring that the organizational goals are met. In the last section you saw how to integrate these organizational goals and weight their importance for all to follow. You now need to track their success.

Because so much data is currently available, you need to determine those measures (metrics) that provide a meaningful measure in achieving success within the organization. This process involves identifying criteria that are important to the organization. Typically decisions are made based on one or two criteria, so the metrics to support the decision process should be kept to a minimum. An approach is described in this chapter for identifying decision criteria and determining their overall importance in the decision process and measuring their success.

Based on identifying the important criteria, then data sources are assessed to determine whether this information can be relatively easily obtained, processed, and maintained. Data should be assessed to determine what level of detail should be maintained for it to be used as a metric to measure success. It may be tracked, for example, on a plant-by-plant basis or rolled up across the organization as a whole. Data can come from both automated sources or from assessments made by experienced executives or experts in the field. The process to establish, track, and maintain metrics and measures of success for an organization provides meaningful information in achieving success and understanding the organization's operations at every level.

1.9 Definition of a Metric

A metric is a standard measure to assess performance in a particular activity. A metric is a composite of measures that yield systematic insight into the state of the process or products and drives appropriate action. Metrics can be composed of both objective data such as historical data reported in a database and subjective data such as expert opinions by senior management or experts in the business.

Metrics are important for a number of reasons. You can use them to defend and justify decisions, to provide objective assessment of progress toward goals, and for problem solving and to validate process improvement. Successful enterprises constantly assess themselves and improve in all dimensions of their enterprise. Metrics provide a foundation for the assessment of success of an activity or enterprise.

A good metric is built upon an organization's missions, goals, and objectives. A metric must be meaningful and understandable for management and workers alike. The best metrics derive naturally from the process in which the data is relevant to the process and its collection becomes part of the process. The metric itself must be easily measurable. The requirement for new systems and data to implement a metric should be minimal because if not, data will not be gathered to support it.

Suppose you have established a corporate objective to improve the company's financial position. Following are metrics you can use to support that objective.

Improve the Company's Financial Position

- **EBIT/EBITDA**—Earnings before interest and taxes, and earnings before interest, taxes, depreciation, and amortization
- **FCF**—Free cash flow; the sum of operating cash flow, financing cash flow, and investment cash flow
- **EPS**—Earning per share; net earnings or profit divided by the total number of shares issued
- **P/E Ratio**—Price to earnings ratio; the price of one share of a company divided by its earnings per share
- **Net Working Capital**—Current assets minus current liabilities
- **Debt Ratio**—Total debt divided by total assets
- **Debt/Equity Ratio**—Total debt divided by shareholder equity
- **Return on Assets (ROA)**—Net earnings divided by total assets
- **Return on Equity (ROE)**—Net earnings divided by shareholders' equity
- **Operating Margin**—Operating earnings divided by total revenue
- **EV/EBITDA**—Enterprise value (price of the share times total shares issued) divided by EBITDA

A number of these are related; that is, Debt Ratio (Total debt divided by total assets) and Return on Assets (Net earnings divided by total assets). Key decision criteria and metrics should be limited to the critical metrics so that they are manageable and definitive goals that specific problem solving and improvement activities can be measured against. A resulting subset of metrics that may be used to measure the improvement of a company's financial position could be EBIT/EBITDA, FCF, EPS, or Debt Ratio.

A company may choose any number of decision criteria and metrics to measure project success and evaluate the achievement of its goals. It is better, however, to measure against a few critical criteria rather than try to measure against interrelated criteria or less critical measures.

1.10 Developing Decision Criteria and Metrics

Numerous private sector and government applications provide us an approach to developing decision criteria and metrics. This approach to metrics development is to relate metrics directly to the accomplishment of the goals and objectives of the organization. This process requires the management team to critically examine goals and objectives to ensure the decisions directly relate to these objectives. Decision makers must first establish the goals and objectives and their relative importance in the final decision process. The development of goals and objectives is mentioned in the previous section.

Decision criteria and metrics are then established to support these established goals and objectives. Group decision-making techniques are also utilized to provide a means for developing the decision criteria and weighting their importance. All the decision makers should have a say in the final selection of decision criteria to ensure objectivity and avoid having dominant personalities overly control the process. The steps involved in this time-tested approach follows:

Step 1. Establish overall objectives and goals.

Step 2. Weight the objectives to determine their importance.

Step 3. Select the decision criteria.

Step 4. Weight the criteria to determine their importance.

Step 5. Develop metrics.

Overall, this approach provides a consistent, traceable, and defensible basis for making decisions. This avoids the "I feel this is what should be done" without any justification. The following is an example of the five steps of this process for developing goals, criteria, and metrics.

1.10.1 Step 1: Establish Overall Objectives and Goals

The first step is establishing objectives and goals for an organization. Goals and objectives are established, noting their common basis and required common theme to represent these objectives. These objectives are then used in the development of the preliminary metrics schema. The initial cut is continued to be refined until a final set of goals and objectives are established that satisfies the group. Group decision-making techniques are used to gain this consensus (see Section 1.6.1).

Through a series of meetings and the use of the Nominal Group Technique, a corporation has arrived at the following senior executive corporate objectives.

- Improve customer management.
- Improve financial soundness.
- Improve market position.
- Enhance technology development.

These objectives may be consistent on a year-to-year basis, or may shift on a yearly basis based on corporate strategy.

1.10.2 Step 2: Weight the Objectives to Determine Their Importance

The goals and objectives are then weighted to assess the relative importance of the selected goals and objectives. Group decision-making techniques are also utilized to facilitate this process. A resulting importance weighting scheme is then developed and reviewed with the decision makers. In each step of the process, the decision makers must understand and agree to the methodologies used in the process.

Table 1.2 is an example of input importance weighting and overall corporate weighting for the four objectives previously identified.

Table 1.2 Example of Importance Weighting by Executives

OBJECTIVE	VP Operations Input	VP Operations Weights	VP Sales/ Marketing Input	VP Sales/ Marketing Weights	VP Customer Management Input	VP Customer Management Weight	Total Input Values	Overall Weight
Max/Improve Customer Management	9	28.10%	10	30.30%	10	33.30%	29	31%
Max/Improve Financial Soundness	6	18.80%	7	21.20%	3	10.00%	16	17%
Max/Improve Market Position	9	28.10%	7	21.20%	7	23.30%	23	24%
Max/Enhance Technology Development	8	25.00%	9	27.30%	10	33.30%	27	28%
TOTAL	32		33		30		95	

1.10.3 Step 3: Select the Decision Criteria

For each of the objectives established in step 1, the group must establish a hierarchy of decision criteria to represent the various objectives. Define the decision criteria so that there is a clear understanding of the criteria used and what metrics will be used to measure the criteria. This definition phase provides the framework for establishing the metrics associated with each of the decision criteria. A "first cut" of the overall decision criteria will be developed, reviewed, and revised as necessary by the decision makers and senior management. Table 1.3 shows an example of the corporate goals with their associated decision criteria and metrics.

Table 1.3 Develop the Decision Criteria

Corporate Objectives	Decision Criteria and Metrics
	Customer Calls
	Customer Turn Over
Improve Customer Management	Customer Satisfaction
	OBIDA
	Free Cash Flow
Improve Financial Soundness	Debt
	Market Share
	Brand Loyalty
Improve Market Position	Ability to Attract New Customers
	First to Market
	Technology Development
Enhance Technology Development	Innovation

1.10.4 Step 4: Weight the Criteria to Determine Their Importance

Team members then weight the criteria established in step 3 for their relative importance in the decision process. Again, use group decision-making techniques to facilitate this process. The team must develop a "first cut" of the decision criteria weights and review and revise their findings to ensure reasonableness. Table 1.4 shows an example of a criteria weighting scheme based on corporate objectives and decision criteria importance.

Table 1.4 Decision Criteria Weighting

Corporate Objectives	Objective Weights	Decision Criteria and Metrics	Decision Criteria Weights	Resulting Criteria Weights
		Customer Calls	20%	6%
		Customer Turn Over	40%	12%
Improve Customer Management	31%	Customer Satisfaction	40%	12%
		OBIDA	50%	9%
Improve Financial Soundness		Free Cash Flow	30%	5%
	17%	Debt	20%	3%
		Market Share	50%	12%
		Brand Loyalty	25%	6%
Improve Market Position	24%	Ability to Attract New Customers	25%	6%
		First to Market	30%	8%
		Technology Development	50%	14%
Enhance Technology Development	28%	Innovation	20%	6%

1.10.5 Step 5: Develop Decision Criteria Metrics

From the decision criteria established in step 3, you can identify the metrics. This involves determining what data to use to measure and quantify the decision criteria. The criteria can be either subjective or quantitative in nature. You can measure criteria using "hard," quantitative data or a subjective scale of the decision makers. Expert opinion can be subjectively used when objective data is not available or when objective data is too costly or time-consuming to obtain. Again, the group must develop a "first cut" of the decision criteria metrics and review and revise its findings as needed to satisfy the decision makers. Table 1.5 shows an example of decision criteria and whether these criteria will be quantified with objective or subjective measures.

Table 1.5 Decision Criteria Definitions

Corporate Objectives	Decision Criteria and Metrics	Definition	Metrics (Objective or Subjective Criteria)
	Customer Calls	Total Monthly Calls to Customer Service Organization	Objective
	Customer Turn Over	Percent of all customers that leave the company	Objective
Improve Customer Management	Customer Satisfaction	Measure of Customer Satisfaction	Subjective
	OBIDA	Operating income before depreciation and amoritization	Objective
	Free Cash Flow	The sum of operating cash flow, financing cash flow and investment Cash Flow	Objective
Improve Financial Soundness	Debt	Debt Ratio - Total assets divided by total liabilities	Objective
	Market Share	Percent of total market held by the company	Objective
	Brand Loyalty	Customers who are repeat buyers	Subjective
Improve Market Position	Ability to Attract New Customers	Assessment of ability to attract new customers	Subjective
	First to Market	Assessment of the number of new technologies that are first to market	Subjective
	Technology Development	Assessment of proficiency of technology development processes	Subjective
Enhance Technology Development	Innovation	Assessment of the ability to innovate	Subjective

1.11 Data Used to Support Metrics

You can use either objective or subjective data to represent metrics used in the decision process. Objective data usually can be described as data that can be quantified by some measure of known commonality. This may be data such as the number of items produced, number of trucks in a location, population of a city, and so on. This data is usually available in some form in company databases and information systems. Typically, statistics such as averages and trends are generated based on a record of this objective data over some period in time. Objective or quantitative data represents a history of activities of a company that has been operating during a given time period.

Qualitative or subjective data can be easily used in a number of different situations. Surveys are good examples of subjective data used to represent a rating of a product or service. Use scales from 1 to 5 or 1 to 10 to represent high, medium, and low assessments for given metrics. Use assessments such as red, yellow, and green in other situations in which individuals (such as military personnel) might find more meaning in rating conditions. Numerical values with their verbal description provide the type of information that can be captured and utilized in a decision model when other information is not available.

Subjective data is data based on someone's opinion or best guess of a condition or a future event. Subjective data is more qualitative in nature in that it defines a situation or condition without specific data points. Subjective data can be generated by individuals within or outside of a company or experts within a given field of operation.

Typically, subjective data or opinions provide insights into a subjective assessment of a metric. Subjective data and expert opinions are typically forward looking in nature trying to predict what will happen in the future. Individuals make assessments based on what has happened in the past and what may happen in the future. Objective data, especially in the form of statistics, however, is based on historical data, thus projecting the future, what has happened in the past, which assumes that the future will behave much like the past. The entire business environment may have changed; thus, what has happened in the past may be a poor representation of the future; thus, a new source of data is required.

Following is a simple scale example that you can use to represent the assessment of the future development potential of a given market.

Future Market Potential

Definition: The projection that this market will become a substantial market in future corporate activities.

Highly Probable	5
	4
Moderately Probable	3
	2
Unlikely	1

This type of information is good information to capture from the experts and decision makers. Utilizing this type of information along with statistics fills gaps that exist to get a better representation of factors that influence future activities.

In developing goals, decision criteria, and constraints, consider a number of parameters in the development process to ensure a set of well-structured, well-represented goals and decision criteria. These development parameters are as follows:

- Goals and decision criteria must represent actual and important considerations in making decisions. Examples would include reducing logistics costs, improving call center response times, and so on.

- Decision criteria must differentiate one project from another in terms of higher or lower priority. This would involve capturing key project characteristics that differ among projects, such as impacts to different functional areas, costs, completion time, and so on.

- Decision criteria must be independent, not overlapping in content or intent, to avoid accounting for the same thought or idea more than once. This tends to overweight the importance of certain criteria. Instances may occur in which both a component cost and a total cost are considered. The component cost would overlap with the total cost value.

- Decision criteria must be defined as clearly as possible to ensure that the decision criteria in the evaluation process are viewed in the same context. Individuals have different perspectives associated with various terms and definitions. The definitions must be clear.

- Measures and scales developed for the decision criteria must be meaningful in the evaluation process and the data to perform the evaluation easily accessible. Objective data provides a basis for a relatively clear scale or measure. The use of subjective criteria requires that the scale components are clearly defined and represent a natural language intention and meaning.

- Constraints that represent types of mixes, qualifiers, and conditions that would be applied to a prioritized list of items must be identified and differentiated from the evaluation decision criteria. You must define the operating parameters. This may be total budget, capacity constraints, and manpower availability. All of these components put bounds around the issue addressed.

1.12 Structure and Definition of the Problem

The steps and analysis described provide a basis for the definition of the problem and structure of the information. The information gathered as part of the analysis performed in the process provides the basis for further development of the example model. This framework is used to illustrate the process and for assessing and developing the required data to be used for the study and selecting the best methodologies to use in the model.

1.13 Key Concepts in Defining the Objectives

Following are the key points of this chapter:

- Groundwork in understanding and defining the problems facing a corporation is essential to bring to light functional areas requiring improvement. They need to determine the scope of functional areas that may be impacted.

- It is necessary to establish corporate objectives to strategically define the direction of a company. This requires consensus among decision makers.

- A corporation has multiple conflicting objectives that require the balancing of cross-function activities.

- Decision criteria and metrics provide quantifiable measures that can be driven down into the corporate decisions so that activities meet the corporate objectives.

- Understanding the data required and data available to support corporate metrics facilitates the measurement of the key metrics and contribution to accomplishing corporate objectives.

- Subjective data or opinions provide insights into a subjective assessment of a metric. Subjective data and expert opinions are typically forward looking in nature, trying to predict what will happen in the future as opposed to statistical analysis that deals with historical data.

- It is important to weight the objectives and metrics across all executives to gain a consensus in the direction of the company.

- Senior executives must be involved in this initial step of the process to establish the corporate objectives that can drive the cross-functional problem solving effort.

2

Explore the Environment

2.1 Chapter Topic

This chapter presents a new approach to integrated corporate planning. Key corporate functions are assessed to determine the closeness of the functional relationships that can be used as a guide to identifying functional areas for improvement. In addition this chapter assesses benchmarking, variability analysis, and budget contributions to expand beyond the relationships to assess how well these functions perform against industry competitors. All these activities provide a high-level integrated approach to determine the relationship between functional areas, identify functional areas of poorer performance, and identify the stability of the metrics associated with each area.

2.2 Key Corporate Participants

The senior executive team has established an executive team of vice presidents and directors to serve as a cross-functional task force for the effort. This information is then used to identify cross-functional opportunity areas for process improvement and problem solving. The executive team is responsible for communicating progress and findings back to the senior executive team on an on-going basis.

2.3 Integrated Corporate Planning

Many different corporate planning methods focus on identifying strategic positioning and future growth objectives and developing plans to accomplish those goals: methods such as focus groups, strategy sessions, interviews, and data analysis. These methods help senior management to determine focus and direction for future activities within a company. As an enhancement to those methods, an approach is included that focuses on problem areas and interrelationships that need to be addressed to determine areas of the company that need to be fixed to move it into a best in class status. From a problem-focused corporate planning perspective, this process consists of the assessment of the relationships between the key areas of a company, an assessment of each of those key areas in terms of their performance against industry benchmarks, and then visually represents these relationships and opportunity areas that need to be included in the analysis to improve company performance.

This analysis consists of a number of steps.

1. **Assess the Scope of the Problem**—In this step, key corporate functions are identified for evaluation. Activities in one functional area may or may not have an impact on other functional areas. Certain functional areas impact all areas of the company such as human resources, which may or may not be included in the analysis.

2. **Develop the Activity Relationship Matrix**—This step captures the interactions between the functions. An assessment is made to qualify those interactions and record them in a matrix and also develop a diagram to provide a visual representation of the strength of interaction between related areas.

3. **Quantify performance with industry benchmarks and performance evaluations**—In this step, the objectives and decision criteria developed previously are used to evaluate the performance of each of the functional areas. This provides an

assessment of relative performance with industry. These metrics are established standards to develop an overall representation of the problems and their benchmark performance with each of the functional areas.

4. **Develop the Activity Relationship Diagram**—This diagram provides a view of the interaction between functions and industry benchmarks and indicates the opportunities for improvement in each of the areas. A relationship convention is used for the diagram, and which functional areas represent the greatest opportunities for improvement.

5. **Determine the variability of the process and financial contribution of the individual functions**—The variability analysis measures the level of control and the performance of key functional areas. The percent of the total corporate budget for each of the functional areas is also assigned to indicate the financial value of improvements of this function. This provides a measure of the performance improvements and its impact to the corporate bottom line and the operational and financial performance.

6. **Identify specific problem areas to improve**—This analysis provides a roadmap to identify specific problem areas in the company to improve and be included in the analysis. This leads to the scope of the analysis and the individual decision criteria and metrics that show the focus areas for issue resolution.

These analysis activities are directed toward an executive-level evaluation of the company and its functions. In many ways, they provide a roadmap for directing the analysis through the management chain. In this corporate environment, resources must be managed to provide the best return on human and monetary capital. The intent of this approach is to provide a high-level integrated view of where to expend these resources for the most improvement. This holistic view can then be used to drill down into specific areas in which problems need to be solved. The integrated view is provided because it is important to represent not only the magnitude of the issues a company may face, but also to provide a representation of the interactions between the key corporate areas. Additionally, this approach avoids a stovepiped view of how to address various company issues and requires a broader view of the interactive nature of company functions.

2.4 Assess the Scope of the Problem

The first step is to identify key corporate functions. Consider a list of functional areas within a corporation in which certain functions cross all functional areas. This may include areas such as Legal, Human Resources, Corporate Communications, and Security. These areas, although they impact all functional areas, may not have the financial and operational impact of other areas. Unless there is a specific functional issue that significantly impacts the organization, the recommendation is to include only those areas that are measurable and are operationally and financially significant to corporate operations.

Following are the department listings:

- Customer Management
- Corporate Communications
- Corporate Strategy
- Customer Management
- Finance
- Human Resources
- Information Technology
- Legal
- Marketing
- Product Development
- Logistics and Distribution
- Sales
- Security

Typically, the following areas would be included in the assessment.

- Customer Management
- Finance
- Information Technology
- Sales
- Marketing
- Product Development
- Logistics

These areas typically represent high-impact, high-dollar value corporate expenditures. In identifying key areas of performance improvement, include those that provide the best operational and financial return on expended effort.

2.5 Develop the Activity Relationship Matrix

When the key areas of the company to be included in the assessment are identified, an Activity Relationship Matrix is developed for these functional areas. The purpose of this is to identify and qualify the relationships between each of the functional areas of the company. So many times, functional areas perform operations and make improvements without the understanding of the impact of these improvements on other parts of the organization. At times, this can be ignored where the management of one function does not care what happens to another function, just so that they can look better in the organization. More times than not, these are unintentional consequences of one part of the organization trying to do the right thing for the company but missing the fact that their efforts may increase costs on another part of the company. This diagram provides a means to communicate these interactions at an executive level.

The rows and columns of the Relationship Chart in Table 2.3 show how company functions relate. The interactions between the various corporate functions are then assessed. Table 2.1 shows the closeness ratings used in the analysis. Each closeness rating is denoted by a value and a line code that will be used in the development of the Activity Relationship Diagram.

The scale in Table 2.1 is used in the assessment.

Table 2.1 Closeness Rating Scale

Closeness Rating

Value	Closeness	Line Code
A	Absolutely Necessary	≡≡≡≡≡
B	Very Important	═══════
C	Important	────────
D	Unimportant	
E	Undesirable	XXXX

In the evaluation process, each corporate function is evaluated against every other corporate function. For example, 1. Customer Management is evaluated against 7. Sales and the relationship between the two in the example is denoted as A (Absolutely Necessary). If specific reasons exist for the various relationship scores, an annotation is included with the alphabetic assessment, and a description such as in Table 2.2 is also included in the assessment.

Table 2.2 Reasons for Closeness Value

Code	Reason
1	Interrelated Processes
2	Shared Resources
3	Same Management Chain

Although it typically requires a small number of assessments, management must discuss these relationships and develop a full understanding of this interrelationship of the activities for each of the functions. An example of the developed relationship chart is shown in Table 2.3.

Table 2.3 Relationship Chart

From

Department Listing	1	2	3	4	5	6	7
1. Customer Management		B	B	B	C	C	A 1
2. Finance			A 1	B	B	B	B
3. Information Technology				A 1	C	C	B
4. Logistics					C	C	B
5. Marketing						B	A 1
6. Product Development							B
7. Sales							

The activity relationship chart, Table 2.3, is developed using Table 2.1, the closeness rating scale, and Table 2.2, the reasons for closeness value, to ensure you understand the factors that influence the interdependencies between each of the corporate functions. These relationships form a foundation for further analysis and the identification of the degree to which it can impact the resolution of various problems.

2.6 Quantify Performance with Industry Benchmarks and Performance Evaluations

After the relationships are assessed, you need to develop key benchmark criteria for each of the functional areas. These criteria are typically included in a company's annual report and are measured across all companies in an industry to compare their performance. Improving performance, improving customer satisfaction, and reducing costs in the functional areas of a company are common goals and objectives of an organization. Decision criteria and metrics that support these common goals are also typically industry benchmarks. The process described in Chapter 1, "Define the Objectives and Identify Metrics," supports the development of the industry benchmarks in this section. Table 2.4 includes a set of industry benchmark metrics that may be included to represent most industries.

Table 2.4 Industry Benchmarks

Functional Area	Benchmarks
1. Customer Management	Customer Calls
	Customer Turn Over
	Customer Satisfaction
2. Finance	OBIDA
	Free Cash Flow
	Debt
3. Information Technology	Financial
	Ordering
	Supply Chain
	Customer
4. Logistics	Order Fulfillment
	Inventory Loss
	Inventory Levels
	Transportation
5. Marketing	Market Share
	Brand Loyalty
	Ability to Attract New Customers
6. Product Development	First to Market
	Technology Development
	Innovation
7. Sales	Business Sales
	Business Profitability
	Consumer Sales
	Consumer Profitability

Each of the criteria associated with the functional areas is assessed to determine how it is performing against these benchmark metrics.

This indicates how well or how poorly the company is doing using the metrics to identify the areas that need work and those areas that are performing well. Table 2.5 shows a simple scale that you can use to perform the assessment that is based on the factual data gathered from the benchmarking analysis and decision criteria assessment. The scale focuses on the magnitude of the issues in each of the areas; the larger the number, the bigger the problem in the area.

Table 2.5 Industry Benchmark Scoring

Score	Performance Against Industry Benchmarks
1	Significantly Better Than Benchmarks
2	Somewhat Better Than Benchmarks
3	Near or at Benchmarks
4	Somewhat Below Benchmarks
5	Significantly Below Benchmarks

The individual metrics are then aggregated or averaged to generate an overall opportunity score. For example, Table 2.6 shows individual benchmark scores in the Finance area for OBIDA, Free Cash Flow, and Debt as 3, 4, and 4, respectively. The aggregated benchmark score for Finance would be the average score of (3+4+4) / 3 = 3.67. This scoring is used to determine the magnitude of the issues associated with this functional area.

Table 2.6 Functional Area Assessments

	Area	Benchmark Performance (1 high–5 low)	Aggregated Benchmark Performance (1 high–5 low)
1. Customer Management	Customer Calls	3	3.00
	Customer Turn Over	3	
	Customer Satisfaction	3	
2. Finance	OBIDA	3	3.67
	Free Cash Flow	4	
	Debt	4	

continues

Table 2.6 Functional Area Assessments, continued

Area		Benchmark Performance (1 high–5 low)	Aggregated Benchmark Performance (1 high–5 low)
3. Information Technology	Financial	4	3.50
	Ordering	4	
	Supply Chain	3	
	Customer	3	
4. Logistics	Order Fulfillment	1	1.75
	Inventory Loss	2	
	Inventory Levels	2	
	Transportation	2	
5. Marketing	Market Share	4	3.67
	Brand Loyalty	3	
	Ability to Attract New Customers	4	
6. Product Development	First to Market	2	2.00
	Technology Development	2	
	Innovation	2	
7. Sales	Business Sales	3	3.00
	Business Profitability	3	
	Consumer Sales	3	
	Consumer Profitability	3	

After the aggregated performance scoring is generated, this can be used in concert with the relationships between the various functional levels to depict the opportunity areas within a company.

2.7 Develop the Activity Relationship Diagram

Incorporating the aggregated benchmarking information with the functional area relationships provides a view of the magnitude of the problems and their interrelated impact areas. Table 2.7 shows the relationship chart coding or assessment that uses different line thicknesses to depict the strength of these in the Activity Relationship Diagram shown in Table 2.8.

Table 2.7 Closeness Rating Definition

Closeness Rating

Value	Closeness	Line Code
A	Absolutely Necessary	≡≡≡
B	Very Important	━━
C	Important	──
D	Unimportant	
E	Undesirable	XXXX

Table 2.8 Relationship Chart

From

Department Listing	1	2	3	4	5	6	7	Aggregated Benchmark Performance (1 high–5 low)
1. Customer Management		B	B	B	C	C	A 1	3.00
2. Finance			A 1	B	B	B	B	3.67
3. Information Technology				A 1	C	C	B	3.50
4. Logistics					C	C	B	1.75
5. Marketing						B	A 1	3.67
6. Product Development							B	2.00
7. Sales								3.00

The diagram in Figure 2.1 shows the relationships between the functional areas, reasons for closeness values, and the magnitude of the issues associated with the individual areas.

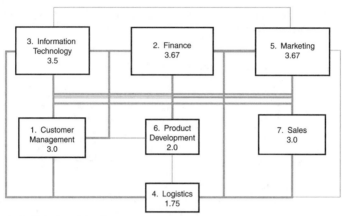

Figure 2.1 Relationship diagram

Both the relationships and the magnitude of the issues associated with each area are shown in the individual blocks. An assessment of 1.0 would show that the company is meeting all the industry benchmarks in each of the key criteria associated with a functional area. An assessment of 5.0 would represent an area that needs significant improvement in a company. The diagram is constructed so that the areas with the greatest need for improvement and the closeness of the functions are shown at the top of the diagram. This creates a visual representation of the areas where management can focus productivity improvement efforts. You need to represent the closeness of the relationships so that the interactions between functions are captured in process enhancements. Corporate knowledge can then be used to identify specific improvement opportunities.

Particular areas to focus on for improvements may be identified from Figure 2.2. In general, areas with the lowest performance and highest relationships may provide key focus areas for improvement within a company. For example, the assessment of Marketing and Finance performance show the greatest potential areas of improvement for the company. There are interrelationships between Marketing and Finance that are strong; that is, Finance, Information Technology, Customer Management, and Sales. Opportunities exist between the lower performance areas and their impacted functions and are grouped together to identify areas in which to pursue improvement. Figure 2.2 shows a grouping of Information Technology, Customer

Management, and Logistics, and Finance, Marketing, and Sales. You can use these groupings to identify areas to pursue to identify projects to enhance corporate performance in an integrated manner.

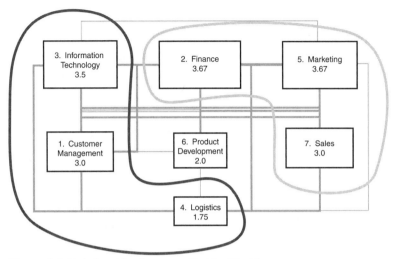

Figure 2.2 Relationship diagram with identified focus areas

2.8 Determine the Variability of the Metrics and Financial Contribution of the Individual Functions

Additional insight can be gained by reviewing other high-level metrics associated with the functional areas. The variability of the performance and the budget of each functional area are assessed. Variability in performance shows the degree of control in each functional area and potential improvement. If the area is performing well, that is, at the industry benchmark level, but has not been performing at this level consistently, the variability can indicate the inconsistency in performance. You can calculate variability using statistical measures or using fuzzy logic techniques to represent the confidence interval associated with the performance area. You can use standard quality control or Six Sigma techniques in variability analysis. Then use these measures to determine whether a functional area may have opportunity for improvement.

The budget associated with a functional area also works to quantify the financial magnitude of opportunity for an area. If a functional area is performing poorly, but is financially smaller in relationship to overall corporate expenditures, it may have a lower priority than other areas. To capture these additional variables, the Relationship Chart is enhanced to include these two different variables and is shown in Table 2.9. Overall, the focus is to identify the corporate areas that have the greatest opportunity for improvement and the most financial impact for improving the operations.

The relationship matrix is used to understand the relationships and connections of each area to another. It is used to identify troubled areas in the company. This analysis marks out the scope and interactions to help determine which areas need to be included in further study. This approach is important because fixing one area may improve another area or worsen performance in another area. You need to understand the holistic view of improvement to ensure that all functional areas are positively impacted by performance improvement efforts.

You can use this information to further identify specific problem areas to improve in the company. This is discussed in the following section.

2.9 Identify Specific Problem Areas to Improve

Company management should address functions across the organization and assess performance against industry benchmarks. Solutions and problems addressed must account for the interactions between the impacted areas. This process then identifies what should be included in the model development process. We have considered the benchmark analysis, looked at a subset of the worst performing areas, and found the poorest performance areas and the scope of where these areas interact. Functional area subcriteria and their associated performance lead to the identification of the scope of opportunity to model for improvement.

Table 2.9 Relationship Chart with Variability and Financial Contribution

From

Department Listing	1	2	3	4	5	6	7	Aggregated Benchmark Performance (1 high–5 low)	Variability: Fuzzy or Statistical	Percent of Total Company Budget
1. Customer Management		B	B	B	C	C	A 1	3.00	Medium	5%
2. Finance			A 1	B	B	B	B	3.67	Medium	10%
3. Information Technology				A 1	C	C	B	3.50	Medium	20%
4. Logistics					C	C	B	1.75	Low	15%
5. Marketing						B	A 1	3.67	High	25%
6. Product Development							B	2.00	Low	15%
7. Sales								3.00	High	10%

The interactions documented in the Activity Relationship diagram provide a basis for developing a problem-centric business process model as discussed in the next chapter. The high-level interactions between functions are evaluated to develop the scope of the problems identified for improvement. The high-level functional interactions are used to ensure that all related processes are captured in the problem-solving effort. The next chapter describes the development of the associated business process models to capture the upstream causes and downstream impacts of related functional improvement areas along with the process for identifying solution opportunities.

2.10 Key Concepts in Exploring the Environment

Following are the key points of this chapter:

- To assess the scope of the problem and opportunities, you need to identify key corporate functional areas to include in the analysis.

- To develop a comprehensive view of corporate performance, you need to identify the interactions, relationships, and impacts between corporate functions.

- Quantifying performance with industry benchmarks and variability analysis provides a measure of the performance of each of the functional areas.

- You can use functional performance along with functional relationships to develop an integrated diagram of corporate performance.

- You can then use this relationship diagram to focus performance improvement efforts on the real problems and their scope.

- The cross-functional executive task force establishes the framework for the cross-functional analysis and assessment. This group of executives also provides feedback to the senior executives on an ongoing basis.

3

Explore the Scope of the Problem and Its Importance

3.1 Chapter Topic

This chapter builds upon the objectives identified and the relationships and performance of the functional areas to identify key problem areas. This analysis not only identifies the corporate issues, but also determines the critical upstream and downstream process and operational impacts associated with improving these processes. Often a fix of one problem can cause an issue in another area. This step ensures that these other area problems are minimized.

3.2 Key Corporate Participants

The project team consists of managers and subject matter experts who model the high-level business processes. The upstream and downstream impacts and the metrics for the opportunity areas are agreed upon. You can use the operational knowledge of other functional managers and experts across the company to determine the causes and effects of many issues. The project manager informs the executive-level task force of the progress in the business modeling development and findings.

3.3 How Does This Fit into the Overall Processes?

After you define the key objectives and metrics associated with the problem you need to have a clear picture and understanding of how this problem and the associated processes fit together. To do so, you need to develop a holistic view of the issues and operating environment in which they exist. This step is one that many individuals fail to perform. Some strategic thinkers can see these interactions and act to solve associated issues without documentation of the issues and processes. However, documentation of the overall business process associated with the issue provides a clear means of communication to those impacted.

The first building block of this process provides a sound definition of the goals and objectives of the company and ways to measure the success of those objectives. The next key is to put all the pieces together and get an overall view of the problem. To do so, you must avoid short-sighted definitions of the problem. The problem that presents itself may not be the actual problem that needs to be solved. More information and an overall view of the environment must be developed to determine the extent of the problem.

An example of this is a case in which an ordering and pricing system for a glass manufacturing company was causing delivery errors. Individuals within the company believed that the delivery company was making errors when delivering to various locations. It was found, however, that the actual problem causing some of the delivery issues was that certain design parameters from the pricing system were not passed to the delivery company's scheduling system. Had the overall process not been reviewed, from the ordering and pricing system to delivery, this issue may have been missed.

3.4 Discussion of Business Process Modeling

When individuals understand the goals, objectives, and measures associated with the problem at hand, it is critical to gain a clear understanding of the true interactions and activities that make up this process.

To understand the problem that is being solved, you must understand the environment in which it is being solved. No activity stands alone in nature, and the inputs, outputs, and interactions between the activity are critical to document.

Unfortunately, you may dread "the business process modeling" sessions—and we can't agree with you more. The problem with business process modeling sessions is that many times, those performing the activity are so engrossed with the actual process that they lose sight of the purpose of the effort. The green block or the red text has little to do with getting to the heart of the matter. High-level, simple representations of the surrounding interactions are more than sufficient to provide the insight needed to understand the various impacts associated with solving the problem. The issue is that many individuals performing these tasks do not have an understanding of what the problem involves. Because of this, they focus more on the process itself rather than depicting the interactions associated with the issue. The business owner or COO must direct those that may be drawing the pictures to ensure that the key critical components of the process are measured.

A high-level business process model provides a roadmap for analyzing the company activities. Sometimes you need to delve into the subcomponents or the sub subcomponents of the problem to discover the issues and answers required to solve the problem. Detail designs associated with components and computer programs do require specific, detailed documentation; however, generally, business processes can be represented with a 20-to-30 block diagram that provides a clear overview. You need to understand where to apply the methods and their purpose and not to become enamored with the solution method itself. The goal is to solve the problem, not to apply a method.

Upper management attitudes can drive operational behavior in identifying certain problems and developing potential solutions. You must be aware that treading on analysis and solutions that may put upper management in a less than favorable light to the organization can be dangerous to a career. Because of this, you must understand the political corporate environment enough to know where and who the potential solutions may impact. Not to say that you should not approach problem solving from a completely analytical and objective position, but you must also know how to present the results in a way that has the best chance of being implemented. This knowledge must guide the problem solver to gain acceptance of the actual solutions by management.

Additionally, you must understand the financial climate of an organization. Are funds available for major or even minor changes? If so, projects can be initiated for system enhancements, construction projects, or new marketing campaigns. If funds are not available, implementable solutions may need to be tempered so that they are low- or no-cost solutions. This adds an additional layer of complexity to the problem solver and the solutions generated.

3.5 What Is the Panoramic View?

How can you get to a panoramic view of the process? Building blocks of objectives, metrics, functional interactions, functional performance, variability associated with the processes, and the overall budget is a functional area that has been developed, but, you must pull together all the pieces into one view of the process. Business process modeling provides a great tool to understanding the holistic picture. From the perspective of this process, this does not mean that every detailed activity is documented. Create a one-page view of the activities, influences, systems, and results that surround this process. This type of process incorporates the following key elements.

- Identification of the problem area and the scope of the Relationship Diagram analysis
- Definition of the sphere of control
- Identification of the key activities, processes, systems, and influences of the problem area
- Upstream and downstream interactions between the areas and activities

- Identification of the data that supports the measurement of the objectives

Figure 3.1 shows a general view of the business process.

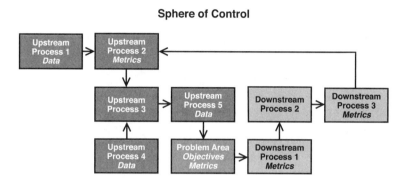

Figure 3.1 Exploring the environment

3.5.1 Identification of the Problem Areas

This step in the modeling process pinpoints the specific problem area that you need to address. The problem was defined in the previous step; however, in this step you need to gain a picture of how this problem fits within the operating environment. The goal is to identify those processes, activities, systems, and influences that surround this problem.

From the assessment in Chapter 2, "Explore the Environment," you identified two different areas of focus. The first is Information Technology, Finance, and Customer Management. The second is Finance, Marketing, and Sales. Using group decision-making techniques (see Appendix A, "Overview of Methodologies"), the executive team has agreed to focus efforts in the area of Information Technology, Customer Management, and Logistics. Figure 3.2 shows the cross-functional focus areas of our example.

Table 3.1 shows the high level metrics, variability associated with processes, and percent of total budget for the areas.

Table 3.1 Functional Area Assessment with Benchmarks, Variability, and Percent of Total Budget

	Area	Benchmark Performance (1 high–5 low)	Aggregated Benchmark Performance (1 high–5 low)	Variability– Fuzzy or Statistical	Percent of Total Company Budget
1. Customer Management	Customer Calls	3	3.00	Medium	5%
	Customer Turn Over	3			
	Customer Satisfaction	3			
3. Information Technology	Financial	4	3.50	Medium	20%
	Ordering	4			
	Supply Chain	3			
	Customer	3			
4. Logistics	Order Fulfillment	1	1.75	Low	15%
	Inventory Loss	2			
	Inventory Levels	2			
	Transportation	2			

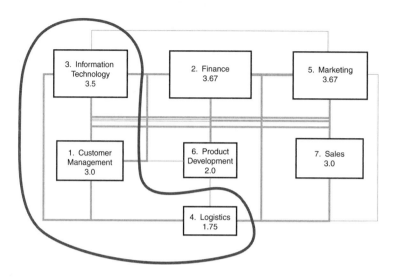

Figure 3.2 Selected cross-functional focus areas

In aggregate, these three functional areas consume 40 percent of the overall budget. The logistics functions appear to be operating above the benchmarks and with relatively low variability; however, they have a significant interaction with Customer Management and Information Technology. Logistics may not be the focus of the improvement efforts, but they must be accounted for in the interaction with systems and customer management.

From a Customer Management perspective, all three areas of customer calls, turn over, and satisfaction have opportunity for improvement. With Information Technology, the financial systems and ordering activities show the greatest areas for improvement.

From this, you can potentially undertake a number of different types of activities to improve operations in these three areas. Create a laundry list of opportunities based on the interactions between the various areas and potential problems that can be solved in concert with other functional areas. For this example, in the problem area you can improve the order management and customer care systems to simplify IT systems, improve customer management, and increase order fulfillment. Based on the current operating procedures within the company, there could be numerous opportunities for improvement.

3.5.2 *Definition of the Sphere of Control*

Understanding the sphere of control is an important step in the process. There may be strategic decisions that drive the problem being solved. The sphere of control, however, may be from the receiving dock in a warehouse to the shipment of finished goods. Your goal is to put a fence around what can and can't be controlled in the solution effort and work to develop the best solution within a viable operating framework.

The activity relationship analysis defines a problem area scope that can impact Customer Management, Logistics, and Information Technology functions. As these problems are further investigated and refined, additional functional areas may be impacted by the identified solutions.

3.5.3 *Identification of the Key Activities, Processes, Systems, and Influences*

In this step, you need to know what activities to include and what to exclude in the holistic representation of the issue. Each of the blocks, as shown in Figure 3.3, may have multiple subprocesses, methods and procedures, and information systems that feed the process. It is critical at this point to represent the overlying functions performed as they interact with the problem at hand. In most cases, it is too easy to get into too much detail too quickly. When that occurs, it is easy for the key elements of the problem to get lost in the detail. You can address these details as necessary as the problem is assessed; however, keep the problem representation at a high but descriptive level so that you can use it to communicate important aspects and results from the effort.

A high-level process diagram has been defined for Customer Management, Logistics, and Information Technology related issues.

3.5.4 *Upstream and Downstream Interactions*

The flow of activities is key to define and model the environment. You must, along with identifying the key activities, understand how these key activities interact with one another and within the identified problem area. The interaction may be the issue, and if this information is not captured, you might lose potentially critical problem solutions.

Customer Management, Information Technology and Logistics

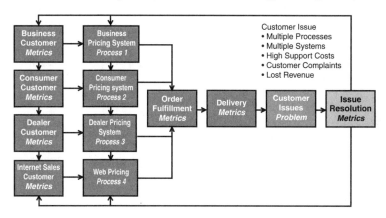

Figure 3.3 Exploring the Customer Management, Information Technology, and Logistics environment

In this example of the glass manufacturing company, multiple types of customers, businesses, consumers, dealers, and web clients exist, each using different ordering and pricing systems and processes to order glass products. Each of the different types of customer have different systems and processes that meet their needs and are called out because of the metrics identified in the Activity Relationship analysis. Order fulfillment and delivery processes are identified but not detailed to minimize the focus on logistics because their performance levels are good. The problem has been identified as Customer Management-related issues and those specifically interacting with the Information Technology system. In this case, you see multiple processes and systems for the different types of customers leading to higher support costs, more customer complaints, and lost revenue. This view leads you to look at opportunities to consolidate and simplify the systems to better support the customers.

3.5.5 *Identification of the Data That Supports the Measurement of the Objectives*

Many of the activities identified as key in evaluating the environment should support the metrics identified by the objectives. It is the relationship of the objectives to the measures that defines what is critical to the success of the effort. Some or all the activity boxes identified in the process should produce data that you can use to evaluate the problem or metrics to measure the success of the effort. This data can provide the insight necessary to develop appropriate solutions and to measure its success.

The metrics identified and gathered in the Activity Relationship Analysis are key to measuring the magnitude and success of the problem-solving effort. Other data and metrics are necessary to understand and analyze the problem. Metrics and data that measure and support the upstream and downstream processes are useful to study various issues. Metrics should be associated with the high-level process blocks identified when exploring the environment.

3.6 Unique Application of Techniques and Methods

Representing the problem in terms of the activities, objectives, data, and metrics provides a high-level view of the puzzle pieces involved in the definition and solution of this unique problem. No one-size-fits-all approach exists that you can use to solve every problem. You need to understand and document each of the components of the problem and how these components fit together to provide the critical framework needed to address the issue.

Just like every problem is different, every solution to the problem is unique. The holistic view of the issue enables you to perform the necessary evaluation to identify the unique solution that meets the requirements of the project. As you move into the assessment phase of the solution development, you can see that the unique problem definition becomes a roadmap to the appropriate evaluation and solution techniques applied to the problem.

3.7 Key Concepts in Exploring the Scope of the Problem and Its Importance

The key points of this chapter are the following:

- Take a holistic view and understand the cross-functional upstream processes and downstream impacts when developing process improvements.

- High-level business process modeling provides a panoramic view of the interactions and impacts in a problem area.

- Understand the corporate objectives and associated metrics so that specific productivity improvement efforts support the corporate goals.

- Understanding a holistic view of the issues and impacted functions provides solutions that support overall corporate objectives.

- The process of going through the solution steps provides a unique insight and benefit to problem understanding and solutions.

- The project team consisting of managers and subject matter experts models the high-level business processes, the upstream and downstream impacts, and the metrics for the opportunity areas. The cross functional knowledge is used to identify and assess the causes and effects of issues facing the organization.

4

Data Mining and Statistical Analysis

4.1 Chapter Topic

This chapter highlights the importance of data analysis. Understanding the problems and determining where improvements should be made is critical. Understanding the information that can quantify and support improvements provides the factual basis for justifying improvements to operations and processes. You learn about a number of methods to analyze data in the Appendices.

4.2 Key Corporate Participants

The project team uses the subject matter experts within the company to analyze the operational data, quantify performance, and identify improvement opportunities. The individuals that perform these functions and generate the originating data should be part of the study team. Findings are communicated to the executive task force.

4.3 Assess the Information and Its Availability

After the structure and the definition of the problem have been determined, the next step is to perform various data and statistical analysis with the available information. So much data is currently available, it is often difficult to sort through the stacks of data to determine what is or is not important. Data can come from automated databases, experts, surveys, work sampling, and various other approaches.

Often the data analysis is all that you need to solve the problem. Other times you can use some data and statistical analysis in the analysis and modeling process. You can use various approaches including the following:

- **Data queries, groupings and summaries**—Database analyses, spreadsheets
- **Statistical analysis**—Mean, standard deviation, variance, regression analysis
- **Forecasting**—Moving averages, exponential smoothing
- **Future predictions**—Expert opinion

The personal computer has significantly enhanced the ability to perform basic data analysis. Spreadsheets and database languages are relatively easy to use and you can use them to perform numerous analyses on available data within a short amount of time. The ability to graph data as well can provide insight into trends and performance of the corporation. Some tools such as Microsoft Windows and spreadsheets have built-in statistical analysis functions that can aid to quickly analyze data and information. You can use forecasting to predict future activities based on the historical data. To predict the future, the use of expert opinion and the judgment of those experts in the field can be one of the best predictors. Artificial intelligence, especially Neural Networks, provides a statistical basis for forecasting future direction. These approaches require large amounts of data but are useful in making future predictions.

One area of model development requires the development of statistical models to measure the variability in a process, such as safety stock levels or service levels. The capability of a company to have various levels of product on-hand directly impacts customer satisfaction for the company. Cost, production, and capacity considerations may impact an organization's capability to meet safety stock requirements. However, the capability or inability to supply product to customers on a timely basis directly impacts part of the bottom line of a company's operation. Statistical analysis and forecasting are important parts of data analysis and model development.

Key in data analysis is to determine what the information can tell you about the operation. Again it is easy to fall into the trap to perform analysis for the sake of the analysis. One example of this is a group within a company that was tasked to perform regression analysis. Unfortunately, the group worked hard with regression analysis but had no context with which to evaluate solutions. It is a perfect example of using a method for the sake of using a method. This analysis within the correct operational context of how the process operates could have helped provide valuable results. However, this group was disbanded because management did not understand how each of these puzzle pieces fit together in the overall operation.

The complexity of the business environment, the objectives to be accomplished by the organization, the availability of data, and the time frame for the development of the model can dictate what methods and analysis you should use to solve the problem. Models may require combining a number of methods, such as multiple objective decision making, statistical analysis, simulation, and expert system technology. The goals and objectives of the decision makers, available data, and the time frame determine the modeling process.

This modeling process involves looking at the whole process, the objectives selected, the metrics and available data, the decisions to be made, the business environment, and the time frame, and then integrating together the information gathered to determine the structure of the problem, the data and statistical analysis, and the methodologies available and best suited to solve the model. The decision maker must understand how the decision process works to become comfortable with the decisions generated because his future and the future of the company depends upon the decision to be made. It is mandatory to keep the decision methods understandable and explainable to the decision maker. Thus, the simpler the method selected, the better. For example, use a simple ranking rather than a complex model such as multiple objective linear programming. This makes the argument that the best method is the one that the decision maker feels comfortable with and uses.

Integrating the data analysis, the solution process, together with the decision maker goals, ensures the model can support the decisions to be made. With the availability of computers, the models developed should be automated to the degree that is feasible. This may include several levels of automation:

- Basic spreadsheet
- Databases
- Databases or spreadsheets integrated with user-friendly front-end screens
- Full computer software systems with data input, data output, processing logic, and reports
- Computer application systems networked within a company or between companies over the Internet

One reason to automate a model is the ability to quickly perform sensitivity analysis. Generating the first answer from a model is only the start of the analysis for decision making. You need to test various parameters and scenarios in the decision process to determine the best solution. Updating the data can keep the model current and representative of the changing business operations. As the business climate changes, the model should be dynamic and adapt to the changing environment.

Today, you can use personal computers with fast processing times and large memory capacity for statistical analysis of a large amount of data that in the past was not possible. Spreadsheets and database languages also have considerable capabilities to analyze and interpret data.

4.4 Data Summarization

After developing an understanding of the problem, the next issues addressed are the goals, criteria, and metrics. You need to know what data is available within the organization to support the analysis. Initially, you should look at the computer systems and information flow used by the organization. These may be production systems, accounting systems, sales data, distribution systems, warehousing data, and so on. The decision analyst should gain a thorough understanding of the information available and its quality throughout the organization. This understanding of the available data and the ease of accessing helps to formulate the appropriate model.

Often, organizations do not realize what information they possess. Individuals within an organization tend to view the data as "their databases." Data from a production system may be useful in understanding other areas of operation such as a shipping or distribution problem. The analysis of sales data should be integral to the production planning process and manpower planning. However, data can be a political time bomb within an organization. Individuals in one division do not want to provide data to another division because of turf issues and potential criticism. Positioning and political savvy are just as important as the actual data analysis, which should always be handled with care.

Different individuals within an organization provide different perspectives about the data in a particular database. The database administrator may simply describe the required data fields and data format. The manager requests the types of reports and frequency that she needs from the system to control the operation. All these pieces of information are worthwhile and beneficial in identifying data that is useful in understanding the process.

Understanding the need for data from various users' perspectives provides insight into the accuracy of the data and decisions being made. A database administrator may feel confident about the majority of the data fields, whereas an end user may indicate that certain data has limited value because of aggregation and timeliness. Understanding what data is available directly affects the precision of the model.

4.4.1 Queries and Summaries

Data can be analyzed in its basic state; that is, the number of items produced in a given hour on a production line, or can be summarized and aggregated to a higher level, such as for the month of February, on average, or x number of items produced on the production line. The level of detail required by the model determines the accuracy of the decision produced by the model.

Two data analysis tools are readily available on most desktop computers: Microsoft Excel, a spreadsheet application, and Microsoft Access, a database application. Both of these application tools have query capabilities and statistical functions that you can use to summarize data and generate useful statistics.

There is no predetermined analysis that should be performed on data. Data analysis is based on understanding the objectives of the model and the availability of the data and the decisions to be made with the model. You need an understanding of the problem before you can perform any beneficial data analysis. Make a number of queries and analyses and scrutinize the data to gain an understanding of the problem and accuracy of the data. One analysis leads to other analyses, which may lead to a direction you had not originally planned.

In the example described earlier, a number of data queries and summaries can provide understanding of the operating processes. For example, the company has various types of customers. These customers are divided into Business, Consumer, Dealer, and Internet Customers. You can use different ordering and pricing systems for each of these different customers. Running a data query is important to determine the issues associated with each customer. Table 4.1 illustrates a query and how it can be useful.

Table 4.1 High-Level Performance Indicators

Customer Type	Total Monthly Orders	Percent of Total Orders	Percent On-Time Fulfillment	Percent On-Time Delivery	Customer Complaints per Thousand Orders
Business	3,000	18.8%	99.7%	99.5%	25
Consumer	5,000	31.3%	99.8%	99.7%	15
Dealer	2,000	12.5%	99.9%	99.9%	5
Internet	6,000	37.5%	99.9%	99.9%	8

This data query shows that orders coming through the business and consumer pricing systems tend to have the lowest on-time fulfillment and delivery levels for the company. Further analysis is required to understand why these two types of customers using these two different pricing systems may cause issues in fulfillment, delivery, and increased customer complaints.

Often, individuals may complain that data in a system is "not good" or "incomplete." Statistically and analytically, this may be true to varying degrees; however, these data sources may be the only data available. Thus, even if incomplete, they can provide valuable insight to problem solving and decision making. If the degree to which data is incomplete can be quantified, that is, "The operator enters only data into the system every hour instead of every half hour," the inconsistencies or incompleteness of the data can be compensated for and be incorporated into the development of the model. It is difficult in most organizations to get people to provide new information, so learning how to utilize existing data sources, even with their problems, usually is extremely beneficial.

4.4.2 Data Groupings

In most companies, large amounts of data are available in one form or another. This data usually provides too much detailed information to be useful to decision makers. If this is the case, you may need to summarize data into logical groupings to provide a better way to present the data and gain a better understanding of the available information. These groupings may simplify the model and thus make it more understandable to the users within the organization.

Although statistics are discussed in more detail in Appendix A, you can use one fundamental theorem in statistics to justify grouping and analyzing data samples. Basically, the normal distribution provides a good approximation to the sampling distribution of the means of a process in which the number of samples is as small as 25 or 30. This may also apply for smaller samples. For random samples from a normal population, the sampling distribution is normal regardless of the size of the sample. Practically speaking, this means that you can use standard, easily understood statistics to represent most data samples. Said another way, the mean of the means of any sample distribution can be approximated by the normal distribution. Using the concept of the "mean of the means" is useful in grouping and analyzing data, as shown in the following example.

An example is based on data gathered for a manpower planning model in which more than 30,000 tasks were recorded as part of a survey in an organization. These 30,000 tasks represented more than 1,500 uniquely individual tasks performed within the organization. To develop a representation of the types of tasks performed, the number of times that they were performed, and the average time it took to perform them, these tasks were grouped into 24 major categories of like type activities meaningful to the organization. Following are examples of these 24 task time categories:

- Provide general administrative support and maintenance.
- Participate in teams, workgroups, committees, and other meetings and teleconferences.
- Develop and maintain information systems.
- Use data management/data entry/data analysis.
- Provide technical, analytical, and operational support.
- Develop and maintain policies and procedures.
- Develop, coordinate, and support major programs, systems, industry-related initiatives.
- Research, coordinate, and perform special projects as required.
- Attend training.

Within the 24 different categories of task times, the average time of the individual tasks performed and the frequency of the tasks were computed. Then the average of the averages (weighted by the frequency of the tasks) were computed to develop an average activity time for each of the 24 task subcategories. Any of the tasks that fell into a task subcategory was then assigned the task time for the task subcategory overall. The average activity times developed for this model were based on the Central Limit Theorem that in essence states that the mean of the means of a sample distribution approaches the standard normal distribution. This approach is statistically valid because of the Central Limit Theorem. This process then reduced the 30,000 tasks into a manageable 24 different groupings of task times with their own statistical distributions that were a logical representation of the work being performed. Each task subcategory had an activity time profile consisting of the following elements:

- Identification of specific activities performed with each one of the 24 subcategories
- The average time it takes to perform an activity in a task subcategory
- The frequency (number of occurrences) of each of the tasks that occur within a specific task subcategory
- A measure of the variability of the average activity time of all the tasks

Another method of grouping data is to develop certain sets of criteria in which items that fall within those parameters become grouped together as part of that set of data. For example, there may be three different sets of parameters, such as the cost of an item, the criticality of an item, and the final assembly. Each part is then placed into a "market basket" that represents a given cost, criticality, and end item for the part. For example, an item might cost $0.50, have a criticality of Medium, and be used in the Item B. All items with costs between $0.00 (figuratively) and $0.99, criticality Medium, and Item B would be in the same market basket or grouping of items. The user can set ranges of data; that is, change the cost ranges, and then group the items based on the three parameters within the model, as shown in Figure 4.1.

Criticality of Item			Cost			End Item		
Low	405		$0.00 – $0.99	180		Item A	400	
Medium	455		$1.00 – $4.99	250		Item B	500	
High	281		$5.00 – $9.99	125		Item C	241	
Total Items	1141		$10.00 – $24.99	209		Total Items	1141	
			$25.00 – $49.99	185				
			$50.00+	192				
			Total Items	1141				

Figure 4.1 Data groupings

This would result in a potential of 6 * 3 * 3 = 54 groups of items or market baskets instead of 1,141 individual items. The type of grouping parameters, cost, criticality, and end assemblies are what individuals can relate to within an organization. Using approaches such as these for grouping data can greatly reduce the quantity of data processed in a model and still maintain enough detail to be meaningful to the decision process. When the results are obtained from the model, they can be decoupled in the same way in reverse order as they were grouped, obtaining the original detailed answer.

4.5 Analysis and Decision Methods

This chapter provides an overview of some of the key techniques in integrated management decisions and traditional data mining and analysis for improving operations. Each of the areas discussed represent entire fields of study. This chapter highlights that these techniques exist and that they should be reviewed when developing decision models and solving organizational problems. These techniques focus on improving the efficiency of an organization and are important in solving real-world problems, as stated here.

- **Statistical analysis**—Summarizes data into defined measures to represent characteristics of the information based on probability theory
- **Forecasting**—Used to predict future occurrences based on historical data
- **Expert opinion**—The use of experience and experts to provide subjective input for data and decision making for future activities that have no history
- **Artificial intelligence**—Sophisticated techniques that attempt to replicate human decision making capabilities
- **Fuzzy logic**—Enables "soft" statistical measures and quantification based on possibility theory in which confidence is set on a range of values within which the value may fall
- **Decision methodologies**—Different methodologies that support and structure decision-making processes
- **Group decision making**—Methodologies that synthesize group opinions into decisions
- **Multiple criteria decision making**—Decisions that rank alternatives based on several objective and/or subjective criteria

- **Multiple objective decision making**—Decisions you can optimize that involve several conflicting goals and trade-offs and are limited by resource constraints

More reading is available for each of these topics in Appendix A.

4.6 Key Concepts in Data Mining and Statistical Analysis

Following are the key points of this chapter:

- Key in data analysis is determining the available information and providing insight into the operation.
- The complexity of the business environment to be modeled, the objectives to be accomplished by the organization, the availability of data, and the time frame for the development of the model will dictate what methods and analyses are required to solve the problem.
- The decision maker must understand how the decision process works to feel comfortable with the decisions generated from a decision model.
- Decision methods must be understandable and explainable to the decision maker.
- The best method is one that the decision maker feels comfortable with and uses.
- The project team utilizes the subject matter experts within the company to analyze the operational data, quantify performance, and identify improvement opportunities. Findings are communicated to the executive task force.

5

Solve the Problem and Measure the Results

5.1 Chapter Topic

After performing the analyses, as shown in Chapters 1 through 4, you need to solve the problem. The data analyses may lead to a clear solution. In other cases, you might need computer-based solutions or more sophisticated methods. The best solution is the one that the decision maker understands and uses. This chapter focuses on determining the best methods that the data and operating environment can support.

5.2 Key Corporate Participants

The project team develops potential improvement alternatives and assesses their viability. Findings need to be communicated to the executive task force.

The process described ensures that decisions are made at each level that supports the corporate goals and objectives. Each of the steps in this process provides definition, structure, and analysis and ensures the decision process is beneficial to the entire corporation. You can glean a great deal of planning information from the modeling process and that enables the decision maker to test the impact of decisions before they are made.

Selecting the proper data, information, and methodologies integrated into a model requires both skill and art. Understanding the overall problem, the information available, and the objectives provides an overall perspective of the organization and how to improve the organization. This entire book has been developed to discuss and explore these concepts. It provides discussions of new and different tools that you can use in this process and shows examples of how to use these tools and processes in a way that previously was not possible.

5.3 Select the Best Method That the Data Can Support

This process involves integrating the information gathered and deciding the structure of the model, the data and statistical analyses, and understanding of the methodologies available that are best suited for the problem. It is fundamental that the decision maker must understand how the decision process works to feel comfortable with the decisions generated by the model. The future of the company may depend upon these decisions. Thus it is necessary to keep the decision methodologies simple, understandable, and explainable. The simpler the method selected the better. For example, use a simple ranking rather than a complex model such as linear programming because the mathematics behind the ranking model are simple and easily understood.

The model should be dynamic and easily adapted to fast-changing business conditions. The methodology selected should utilize readily available data and information. Some models are developed that require a significant effort to collect the data and maintain the model. If this occurs, more time is spent updating the data and the model rather than using the model to evaluate decisions. If it is too difficult to maintain a model, the model will quickly be forgotten.

The complexity of the business environment, the objectives, the availability of data, and the time frame for the decisions dictate what methods are best used to solve problems. Some models may require multiple criteria methodologies for their solution (see Appendix A and B). Others may require incorporating several methods such as multiple objective decision making, statistical analysis, simulation, and expert systems. The goals and objectives of the decision makers can eventually point to the techniques to be used and the structure of the modeling process.

5.4 Model to Represent the Decision Process

Many different methods exists that you can use in the decision process such as ranking, variability analysis, critical path, work design methods, simple additive weights, group decision making, fuzzy logic, linear programming, and multiple objective decision making. From the scope of the problem, the depth of the issues, and the available data, you select the methods that fit the problem.

In the glass manufacturing example we discussed in the previous chapter, customer issues have been identified, and key metrics associated with operational characteristics have been identified. Table 5.1 shows that there are four different ordering and pricing systems related to customer activities. There are issues with the Business and Consumer orders in on-time fulfillment, delivery, and customer complaints. Solutions are proposed and are investigated that incorporate Customer Management, Logistics, and Information Technology functions as shown in Table 5.1.

Table 5.1 Performance Indicators Targeted for Improvement

Customer Type	Total Monthly Orders	Percent of Total Orders	Percent On-Time Fulfillment	Percent On-Time Delivery	Customer Complaints per Thousand Orders
Business	3,000	18.8%	99.7%	99.5%	25
Consumer	5,000	31.3%	99.8%	99.7%	15
Dealer	2,000	12.5%	99.9%	99.9%	5
Internet	6,000	37.5%	99.9%	99.9%	8

An analysis was performed to determine the primary reasons why these issues were higher with the business and consumer customer types and pricing systems. The goal of the analysis was to determine the underlying issues that cause a lower performance level with the business and consumer customers. Additionally, as part of this process, we looked to perform this analysis from a cross-functional perspective, understanding the interactions between our three key areas of focus. Data was gathered and the five whys were asked to arrive at the cause of the problems. In our case, the four computer systems had different system parameters, which enabled different combinations of parameter selections. Specifically, incorrect combinations of order fulfillment parameters were allowable in certain instances in the business and consumer systems. This analysis leads to corrective action recommendation that computer systems be updated to reduce these errors instead of relying on the existing training procedures to avoid these errors.

A number of different alternatives were developed to remedy the issues. Funding is tight; therefore, not all potential solutions can be implemented. Following is a list of alternatives.

- Modify the business pricing system to eliminate errors.
- Modify the consumer pricing system to eliminate errors.
- Reduce the number of ordering and pricing systems to two systems in which the business, consumer, and dealer systems would be the same system, and the Internet system would remain the same.

An economic analysis was performed to determine the life cycle costs associated with each of these alternatives. Investment costs would be required; however, savings in delivery charges, streamlining support functions, and reducing customers leaving the company would greatly benefit the company.

In addition, decision criteria were identified to evaluate which of the alternatives would best meet the corporate objectives. The decision criteria and corporate benchmark metrics identified in Section 1.10 are used as the basis for developing the decision criteria. These decision criteria from Section 1.10 are shown again here in Table 5.2.

Table 5.2 Corporate Decision Criteria and Metrics for Evaluating Performance Improvement

Corporate Objectives	Decision Criteria and Metrics
Improve Customer Management	Customer Calls
	Customer Turn Over
	Customer Satisfaction
Improve Financial Soundness	OBIDA
	Free Cash Flow
	Debt
Improve Market Position	Market Share
	Brand Loyalty
	Ability to Attract New Customers
Enhance Technology Development	First to Market
	Technology Development
	Innovation

The decision criteria derived from these benchmark criteria and used in our analysis of alternatives are shown next. Many times, too much information is captured and maintained. These benchmark criteria were selected in the evaluation because they target performance measures that impact performance.

- Development Cost
- On-Time Fulfillment
- On-Time Delivery/Transportation
- Customer Calls
- Customer Turnover
- Economic Benefit

These decision criteria were used to develop an evaluation matrix to rank the different alternatives. The method of simple additive weights was used to score each of the alternatives with the decision criteria, weight the decision criteria, and rank the alternatives. The results are shown in Table 5.3, and the cost and priority used to scale the input values is shown in Table 5.4.

Table 5.3 Evaluation of Alternatives Using the Simple Additive Weighting Method

Alternatives	Development Cost	Development Cost (Scale)	Fulfillment Improvement (Scale: 1 (low)– 5 (high))	Delivery Improvement (Scale: 1 (low)– 5 (high))	Customer Call Improvement (Scale: 1 (low)– 5 (high))	Customer Turnover Improvement (Scale: 1 (low)– 5 (high))	Economic Benefit (Scale: 1 (low)– 5 (high))	Score
		10%	15%	15%	25%	25%	10%	
1. Modify the Business Pricing System	$2,000,000	3	2	3	3	3	2	2.75
2. Modify the Consumer Pricing System	$2,500,000	2	2	3	3	3	2	2.65
3. Reduce the Number of Pricing Systems	$6,000,000	1	4	4	4	4	5	3.8

Criteria Importance Weight

Table 5.4 Development and Economic Benefit Scoring Scale

Development Cost Scale
5: Very low <$500K
4: Low >=$500K to <$1M
3: Medium >=$1M to <$2.5M
2: High>= $2.5M to <$5M
1: Very high >=$5M

Even though the alternative to reduce the number of ordering and pricing systems costs the most, it has the highest overall financial and operational benefits. The recommendation would be to consolidate the different pricing systems and reduce the number of systems from four systems to two systems to improve customer satisfaction and reduce overall costs for the organization.

5.5 Model Automation

After the metrics, the structure, the data and statistics, and the methodology have been selected, they are then integrated into a decision model. The decision model should be as automated as reasonably possible so that it can be easily utilized on an ongoing basis. The degree to which a model is automated should be based on the end users and their understanding of the decision process. Do not develop a system that is easily used but hides the actual analysis from the decision maker. The number of users and the access to the model dictate where it should reside; for instance, on a single machine, a company network, or the Internet. Following are some suggestions for computer tools that may be useful for some decision situations.

- **Basic spreadsheet**—Use a basic spreadsheet for statistical models and data models. Statistical and data analysis capabilities exist within a spreadsheet, and most people easily understand them. Use macros to program basic screen functions and generate analyses to assist the user. Although the spreadsheet is easier to use, it does not have the computational capabilities that more sophisticated models require.

- **Databases**—Use databases with simple queries and macros to automate basic decision models. Again, the level of sophistication of the model is minimal, however; it may be sufficient for solving the problems at hand. This type of model would focus primarily on the use of queries or Standard Query Language (SQL) statements to generate the various summary data and metrics.

- **Databases or spreadsheets with front-end screens**—Build user interfaces into the model using database languages for spreadsheets on a limited basis. They provide an additional level of ease to access the data. Use programs such as Microsoft Access and Microsoft Excel to develop user interfaces and menu options within the decision model. Additionally, use programming languages such as Visual Basic or Visual C++ or other object-oriented languages to build sophisticated computer screens that you can design for specific user needs.

- **Complete computer application systems with data input, data output, and processing logic**—A complex decision model that has a number of capabilities requires the development of a customized computer application to support the model. Data input screens, data output screens, processing logic, and database support are required as necessary. Also, develop reports to provide the decision maker with the type of analysis and output required to make decisions in a timely manner. These applications can differ in complexity based on end user requirements and the sophistication of the user. Many times you can develop prototypes with Microsoft Access that then lead to a fully developed computer decision support system.

- **Computer application systems on a company network**—Depending upon the number of users, you can develop a network-based decision model that is accessible through a company network. Develop the model so that a number of individuals can simultaneously use the system. More rigorous design, development, and testing would be required for a system that is networked to a larger audience.

- **Computer applications are available from the Internet**—You can also use computer applications and websites to access decision models. Two categories of these applications would include those Internet applications that simply present "canned" or prerun data or metrics and those Internet applications that provide interactive decision analysis. Some simplistic examples of this may be an Internet site that displays the latest car models for a car manufacturer without query capabilities. This could be compared to an Internet site that provides users with the ability to input criteria for an automobile such as make, year, color, and gas mileage and then present all the cars available and their prices that satisfy these criteria. This approach is applicable for individuals in remote locations.

Automate a model only to the degree that it is beneficial in its overall use. For example, a small model used infrequently to make decisions on a local level should not be automated in the same way as decision applications accessible to a national user base. The development of a decision model must be cost effective and consider the time and resources available.

5.6 Key Concepts to Solve the Problem and Measure the Results

Following are the key points of this chapter:

- The best method is the one that the decision maker understands and uses.
- The model should be dynamic and easily adapted to fast changing business conditions.
- The methodology selected should utilize the data and information that are readily available.
- A decision model should be automated so that it can be easily used and updated on an ongoing basis.
- The project team develops various improvement alternatives and assesses which is most viable.

6

Evaluate the Results and Do Sensitivity Analysis

6.1 Chapter Topic

This chapter discusses how to use the decision model to explore the results and determine their economic viability. A well-defined model needs the functional capability to change key parameters and constraints and determine the impact of those changes on the final solution. What-if analysis is a key ingredient in the decision process. The first solution is not necessarily the best solution. You must test the sensitivity of the variables in the solution to ensure that you reach the best solution.

6.2 Key Corporate Participants

The project team uses sensitivity analysis and what-if analysis to test and analyze the improvement alternatives. After you explore the potential solutions, you can present the results to the executive task force that then can select the best solution.

6.3 Measure the Degree of Success

The previous chapters described the components associated with the decision model. This chapter discusses how the information developed in this process is integrated into a decision model and then used in the decision-making process. As has been stated previously, going through this analysis process can provide decision makers with data and information to improve the decision making process whether or not a model is developed. This chapter discusses how you can monitor the analyses previously performed and integrate it into an automated decision model to use throughout the organization on an on-going basis.

In this example, the suggested changes have been made to reduce the number of ordering and pricing systems for a glass manufacturer from four to two systems. Table 6.1 shows high-level performance metrics of an improvement in each of the critical areas identified. The percent of on-time fulfillment for each of the customer types has improved by 0.1 percent. The percentage for on-time delivery has improved to 0.2 percent. The number of customer complaints per thousand orders has been reduced from 25 to 15 for business customers and from 15 to 8 for consumer customers. Although the percentages are small, the impact to overall orders is great because of the number of monthly orders.

Table 6.1 Performance Improvements

Customer Type	Total Monthly Orders	Percent of Total Orders	Percent On-Time Fulfillment	Percent On-Time Delivery	Customer Complaints per Thousand Orders
Business	3,000	18.8%	99.8%	99.7%	15
Consumer	5,000	31.3%	99.9%	99.8%	8
Dealer	2,000	12.5%	99.9%	99.9%	5
Internet	6,000	37.5%	99.9%	99.9%	8

Additionally, look at any changes to the benchmark metrics. Improvement in the area of customer calls and pricing systems has also been realized. Specifically, customer calls under the customer management function and ordering under the information technology function have both improved their benchmark scoring by one point.

This has improved benchmarks in both of these functional areas. The benchmark metrics are high-level corporate wide metrics. Improvement in one area may not lead to significant overall improvement with the company. However, incremental changes can lead to significant overall improvement of company performance.

A benefit of this approach is that it forces changes to corporate performance across multiple company functions. Functional areas 1, 3, and 4 are the most impacted of the five functional areas analyzed and are included in Table 6.2.

6.4 Economic Analysis

You must assess the cost of activities within an organization to understand the economic impact of processes, operations, and investments. Costs may be fixed, variable, reoccurring, or have one-time investment costs. Additionally, you must also include costs associated with ongoing maintenance, operations, repair, and disposal when analyzing problem areas. From a holistic perspective, include life cycle costs from inception to disposal. Project management and life cycle costing methodologies work to capture the entire set of related costs associated with an activity. These costs extend to marketing, training, disposal, overhead, and others, which are not normally accounted for in the evaluation process.

You can use a Cost Breakdown Structure tool to ensure that you capture all the associated costs with a project or activity. This hierarchical diagram identifies typical costs found in a variety of different type of improvement activities or projects. There are four major categories of costs: Research and Development, Investment, Operations and Maintenance, and System Phase-Out and Disposal (Fabrycky and Blanchard, 1992). Capture project costs by category and year to account for each type of cost. Figure 6.1 shows a corporate level diagram of a Cost Breakdown Structure.

Table 6.2 Functional Area Benchmark Improvements

Functional Area Assessment with Benchmarks, Variability, and Percent of Total Budget

Area		Benchmark Performance (1 high–5 low)	Aggregated Benchmark Performance (1 high–5 low)	Variability–Fuzzy or Statistical	Percent of Total Company Budget
1. Customer Management	Customer Calls	2	2.67	Medium	5%
	Customer Turn Over	3			
	Customer Satisfaction	3			
3. Information Technology	Financial	4	3.25	Medium	20%
	Ordering	3			
	Supply Chain	3			
	Customer	3			
4. Logistics	Order Fulfillment	1	1.75	Low	15%
	Inventory Loss	2			
	Inventory Levels	2			
	Transportation	2			

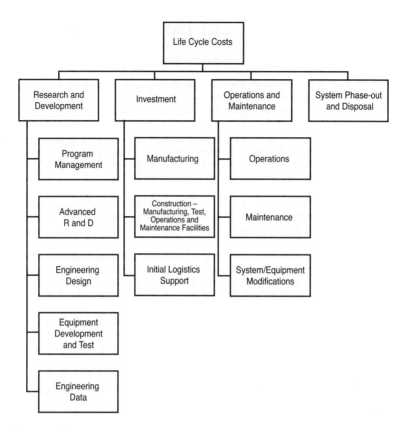

Figure 6.1 Cost Breakdown Structure

You can incur costs at a point in time and at a specified interest rate. You can also generate revenues and cost savings at a point in time. Use these cash flows or series of inflows and outflows of cash over time to measure the profitability of a given activity. Use the time value of money and economic equivalence to measure the inflows and outflows of cash and provide a point of comparison for these measures. Typically, you use the Net Present Value, Rate of Return, or Payback Period to measure the profitability of the project. Numerous books and texts address these important concepts for the analyses of the use of corporate resources. You must account for these economic considerations when determining various courses of action.

6.5 What-If and Sensitivity Analysis

The first answer generated from a decision model is usually the starting point of the decision-making process. A well-defined model has the functional capability to change key parameters and constraints and determine the impact of those changes on the final solution. What-if analysis is a key ingredient in the decision process. In many ways, the information gathered, analyses performed, and models developed all lead to understanding the impact of the decisions made in the changing operating environment. Not only should what-if analysis be performed with the completed model, but it also should be a primary use of the model.

For example, you can easily change budget levels in a resources allocation model because available resources can change at any time. Additionally, the decision maker may want to test funding scenarios with different budgets to determine what projects are the best to be funded now with limited resources. You normally build this what-if analysis into a decision model.

You can see another example of what-if analysis capabilities in the development of a staffing model. In this example, environmental characteristics or workload drivers impact the amount of work that an individual can perform in a given year. The decision model should enable the user to change the workload so that the decision makers can determine whether a new workload estimate is going to change staffing requirements.

Use sensitivity analysis to determine the degree to which various variables and parameters in the model can change and their impact on the solution. This helps determine the sensitivity of solutions to the variability of the data. Having the ability to perform sensitivity analysis is important to determine the range of parameters that can cause changes in model outcomes. This gives you insight to the accuracy of the data and the variability of parameters and establishes confidence in the results. Both what-if analysis and sensitivity analysis are extremely important capabilities and are the main reasons to build decision models.

In this example, you analyze the potential changes to the course of action with the ordering and pricing systems by performing what-if and sensitivity analysis. Use the Simple Additive Weights method to select which of the pricing system projects should be pursued. Suppose that budgets are limited and it is important to complete a project with minimal investment. The importance of a low development cost is key where 50 percent of the overall decision should be based on the development cost, as shown in Table 6.3. If this is the case, the course of action is different, and the best choice is to modify the business pricing system.

If you want to test the sensitivity of your decision, look at what it would take to change the selection based on the improvement of various decision criteria. In this case, look at what it would take to make the modification of the consumer pricing system your selected course of action. The anticipated number of calls from customers, customer turnover, and the economic benefit would need to improve to make the consumer pricing system project your selection. You can perform sensitivity analysis testing individual decision criteria or testing changes to a number of decision criteria simultaneously. In this case, improvements in customer calls, customer turnover, and economic benefit for the modification of the customer pricing system would cause this option to be the best course of action to pursue. Table 6.4 shows the results where we would now select the consumer pricing system in lieu of the business pricing system.

Table 6.3 What-If and Sensitivity Analysis—Changing Importance Weights

| | | Criteria Importance Weight | | | | | | |
| | | 50% | 5% | 5% | 15% | 15% | 10% | |
Alternatives	Development Cost	Development Cost (Scale)	Fulfillment Improvement (Scale: 1 (low)–5 (high))	Delivery Improvement (Scale: 1 (low)– 5 (high))	Customer Call Improve- ment (Scale: 1 (low)– 5 (high))	Customer Turnover Improvement (Scale: 1 (low)– 5 (high))	Economic Benefit (Scale - 1 (low) to 5 (high))	Score
1. Modify the Business Pricing System	$2,000,000	3	2	3	3	3	2	2.85
2. Modify the Consumer Pricing System	$2,500,000	2	2	3	3	3	2	2.35
3. Reduce the Number of Pricing Systems	$6,000,000	1	4	4	4	4	5	2.6

Table 6.4 What-If and Sensitivity Analysis—Analyzing the Impact of the Evaluation Scores

| | | | | | Criteria Importance Weight | | | |
Alternatives	Development Cost	10% Development Cost (Scale)	15% Fulfillment Improvement (Scale: 1 (low)–5 (high))	15% Delivery Improvement (Scale: 1 (low)–5 (high))	25% Customer Call Improvement (Scale: 1 (low)–5 (high))	25% Customer Turn=over Improvement (Scale: 1 (low)–5 (high))	10% Economic Benefit (Scale: 1 (low)–5 (high))	Score
1. Modify the Business Pricing System	$2,000,000	3	2	3	3	3	2	2.75
2. Modify the Consumer Pricing System	$2,500,000	2	2	3	5	5	4	3.85
3. Reduce the Number of Pricing Systems	$6,000,000	1	4	4	4	4	5	3.8

6.6 Key Concepts to Evaluate the Results and Do Sensitivity Analysis

Following are the key points of this chapter:

- A well-defined model has the capability to change key parameters and constraints and determine the impact of those changes on the final solution.

- Not only should "what-if" analysis be performed with the completed model but it also should be a primary use of the model.

- The first solution is not necessarily the best solution.

- Define an optimal solution as doing something better than has previously been done according to the established goals.

- The information gathered, analyses performed, and models developed all lead to understanding the impact on decisions made in the changing operating environment.

- You must evaluate the cost of activities within an organization to understand the economic impact on processes, operations, and investments.

- Use the time value of money and economic equivalence to measure the inflows and outflows of cash and provide a point of comparison for these benchmarking measures.

- The project team uses sensitivity analysis and what-if analysis to test and analyze the alternative improvement opportunity as directed by senior management. After the potential solutions are explored, present results to the executive task force and senior executives; then they can select the best solution.

7

Summary of Part I

7.1 Summary of Integrated Approach

Part I describes the overall process to ensure that decisions are made to support the overall goals and objectives throughout the organization. Each of the steps in the process provides definition, structure, and analysis to ensure you make the best decisions. The analyses provide insight into how the company operates, its objectives, and its goals. To summarize, following are the key steps involved in this process:

- **Define the objectives**—Ensuring that you establish objectives so that the solutions and performance enhancements support those objectives. You will take a number of steps to develop the corporate objectives that everyone agrees with and weights the importance of each.

- **Solving the right problem**—Determining the correct objectives and goals of the organization, what are the fixed and variable constraints and goals, who are the key decision makers, and what are the decisions to be made.

- **Measuring success in accomplishing the objectives**—Determining the metrics to measure the degree of success in achieving the overall mission and goals, and to measure the decision criteria in the decision process.

- **Integrated corporate planning**—Using a new methodology that takes a high-level view of the interactions of various functions within the company, the key metrics that define the performance of the functions, the benchmark performance of these functions with respect to other companies in the same industry. This holistic view promotes the perspective that decisions in one area impact other functional areas in corporate operations. Additionally, you develop a visual representation of functional performance and interactions to focus executives on the scope of cross-functional solutions and their performance enhancements.

- **Determine the scope of the problem**—Identifying problems in areas of the company recognizing upstream contributors and downstream impacts. Use high-level business process modeling to identify these impacts. Typically, you provide a cross-functional view to identify and measure these interactions and impacts as part of the solution.

- **Data mining and statistical analysis**—Analyze available data and extract as much information as possible from the data that is currently available in order to make decisions using this data along with expert opinion. Explore decision methodologies to determine which methods are most appropriate for use in the decision model environment and ensuring the model is dynamic and easily changed.

- **Solve the problem**—Applying the available solution methods using the ones most suited for the problem being solved in the current business environment and with the available data. Finally, select the best method for the problem that the decision makers can implement. Integrate the various components of the model together into some form of an automated system so that the model can be easily used and changed on an on-going basis (see Appendix A and B).

- **Evaluate the results and do sensitivity analysis**—Evaluating the possible outcomes associated with a decision. Often, the first answer is not the best answer. Sensitivity and what-if analyses provide those tools to evaluate the impact of a decision on the corporate operations. You need to perform an economic analysis to determine the overall financial benefits of the project and have confidence that this is the right solution.

These basic steps and methods provide a framework to solve real-world problems that support the objectives at all levels of an organization. You need to go through the steps presented and engage the appropriate level of management at each of the steps. Going through the steps provides an organized way to analyze the business and identify improvement opportunities that you have not previously identified. Identify the goals and objectives first in building the decision model and then use them to establish the metrics to measure the success of the decisions. This approach then sets up the framework so that the results generated support the goals of the entire organization.

This approach has been used in the development of numerous real-life commercial and government applications and has proven to be successful ensuring the acceptability of the solutions by management. The chapters in Part II, "Case Studies," show a number of applications of this process in a variety of actual case studies.

Part II

Case Studies

8

Logistics Service Provider

8.1 Introduction

This case study assesses a company that is a full-service supply chain provider. This company is owned by a parent company, but functions as a completely separate business unit with its own independent president, board of directors, operating capital, and business processes. The parent company uses this division as its full-service provider; however, it has structured this business unit so that if it does not provide adequate service at a low price, this business unit can be sold off, and a higher performing business unit can be bought in its place. This structure is designed to ensure that the logistics business unit is competitive with the industry.

The parent company sells high-dollar construction equipment throughout the world. The company services both the commercial and military sector. Availability of equipment is critical to meet changing demand, so demand planning, forecasting, inventory investment, and time to market is crucial. Many of the pieces of equipment have long lead times to produce. The company sells equipment on a contract basis and also rents this equipment on an as-needed basis.

Supply chain business unit management understands the need to be competitive and, therefore, knows that it needs to improve in a number of areas to perform at industry standards or higher. Because of this, they have decided to employ the previously described methodology to improve their profitability in the overall operations.

8.2 Define the Objectives

In this scenario, there are multifaceted objectives that the supply chain business unit must meet with the parent company. The business unit must provide high-level performance and low-cost business solutions. The business unit must also help to support the objectives of the parent corporation as a whole. Knowledge of both the parent company objectives and the business unit company objectives must be integrated to successfully operate the combined businesses.

Additionally, the company needs to have a clear understanding of the existing operations, systems, and processes to know current performance levels and what needs to improve so that the business unit provides high-quality services to the parent company and other clients. Multiple facilities are operated by the business unit. Currently, a number of other companies use the supply chain services. Operating performance differs at the various facilities and differs for the various companies that contract these services. These operations must not only meet the parent company's requirements, but also must be flexible enough to contract these supply chain services to other companies to improve their performance levels.

Multiple key stakeholders must be involved to determine corporate objectives. These stakeholders would include at a minimum sales, marketing, operations, information technology, and finance personnel from the corporation. Executive leadership, especially from the functional areas of operations, finance, information technology, and sales personnel need to be engaged in this process. In all, the business unit's success relies on the parent company success and its capability to perform and be profitable and to market its services to other companies. Problems existing within the business unit impact the capability for many different organizations to achieve their goals. Equally important is that the related functional areas may be significantly contributing to the problems that exist in the business unit because of the close operating ties, system interfaces, processes, and requirements. Upstream impacts and downstream results must also be considered if there are interactions of the functions.

Overall, a number of key areas exist that both the parent company and the subsidiary would like to see improved.

- **Operational performance**—This involves ensuring that customers have the right product at the right time.

- **Financial performance**—The parent company wants the business unit profitable, maintaining good customer service, minimizing inventory levels, and minimizing operating costs.

- **Sales**—The business unit wants to grow the business. There is a growing market for outsourcing, and it wants to be a leader in the field.

- **Information technology**—It is critical these days that information passes seamlessly from one corporation to another. Electronic data interchange and direct system interfaces are important to provide real-time information for operations and sales.

These general objectives can be translated into specific objectives and measured to evaluate the progress of improvement in an organization.

8.3 Developing Decision Criteria and Metrics

The following steps have been used to develop the overall objectives, decision criteria, and metrics for the analysis.

8.3.1 Step 1: Establish the Objectives and Goals

Through executive meetings and the use of group decision-making techniques, the general objectives were translated into specific metrics for the business unit. In this case, the following general objectives were agreed upon by the executive group:

- Improve operational performance
- Increase profitability
- Increase sales
- Enhance information technology performance

8.3.2 Step 2: Weight the Objectives to Determine Their Individual Importance

Group decision-making techniques were used to develop importance weighting by the executive group. Each executive was asked to assign percentages of importance for each of the four objectives. Table 8.1 shows the results.

Table 8.1 Importance to Weight of Corporate Objectives

Corporate Objectives	#1 Objective Weights	#2 Objective Weights	#3 Objective Weights	#4 Objective Weights	#5 Objective Weights	Overall Objective Weights
Improve Operational Performance	30%	25%	20%	40%	50%	33%
Increase Profitability	30%	25%	30%	20%	15%	24%
Increase Sales	20%	25%	20%	20%	15%	20%
Enhance Information Technology Performance	20%	25%	30%	20%	20%	23%

The exercise shows that holistically, all the executives believe that improving operational performance is most important. They also believe that improving sales is of lesser importance than the other objectives. The company can use this information in the decision process to determine which areas should be pursued.

8.3.3 Step 3: Select the Decision Criteria

Each of the previous objectives has a number of decision criteria that the company can use to measure and support achieving the agreed-upon objectives. Industry benchmark criteria are beneficial in the development of the decision criteria to have an easily measurable framework for assessing performance that can be communicated to executives, the board of directors, and to the employees. Based on an understanding of the problems to be solved, the following decision criteria have been established for each of the objectives. Table 8.2 shows this information and the average weights.

Table 8.2 Establish the Decision Criteria

Corporate Objective	Objective Weight	Decision Criteria and Metrics
Improve Operational Performance	33%	Warehouse Cycle Time
		On-Time Performance
		Inventory Turnover
Increase Profitability	24%	Warehousing Cost per Unit
		Transportation Cost per Unit
		Inventory Investment
Increase Sales	20%	Market Share
		Market Opportunity
		Sales Growth
Enhance Information Technology Performance	23%	System Reliability
		System Interfaces
		Flexibility

8.3.4 Step 4: Weight the Criteria to Determine Their Importance

The executive group can weight the decision criteria to determine their importance. This provides additional focus for selecting the actual problem areas that should be studied for improvement.

Table 8.3 Decision Criteria Weighting

Corporate Objectives	Objective Weights	Decision Criteria and Metrics	Decision Criteria Weights	Resulting Criteria Weights
Improve Operational Performance	33%	Warehouse Cycle Time	30%	10%
		On-time Performance	40%	13%
		Inventory Turnover	30%	10%
Increase Profitability	24%	Warehousing Cost per Unit	40%	10%
		Transportation Cost per Unit	20%	5%
		Inventory Investment	40%	10%

continues

Table 8.3 Decision Criteria Weighting, continued

Corporate Objectives	Objective Weights	Decision Criteria and Metrics	Decision Criteria Weights	Resulting Criteria Weights
Increase Sales	20%	Market Share	35%	7%
		Market Opportunity	35%	7%
		Sales Growth	30%	6%
Enhance Information Technology Performance	23%	System Reliability	30%	7%
		System Interfaces	50%	12%
		Flexibility	20%	5%

8.3.5 Develop Decision Criteria Metrics

Each of the metrics identified is used in the performance assessment of each of the objectives. In this case, most of the decision criteria are industry benchmarks. Other subjective decision criteria can be used based on expert opinion and industry knowledge. Table 8.4 shows whether the decision criteria (industry benchmarks) are objective or subjective data.

Table 8.4 Definition of the Decision Criteria and Metrics

Corporate Objectives	Decision Criteria and Metrics	Definition	Metrics (Objective or Subjective Criteria)
Improve Operational Performance	Warehouse Cycle Time	Average time to process and order through the warehouse	Objective
	On-time Performance	Percent of time a customer receives product on time	Objective
	Inventory Turnover	Measure of inventory turns per month	Objective
Increase Profitability	Warehousing Cost per Unit	Average cost to process one unit in the warehouse	Objective
	Transportation Cost per Unit	Average cost to deliver one unit to the customer	Objective
	Inventory Investment	Monthly inventory investment	Objective

continues

Table 8.4 Definition of the Decision Criteria and Metrics, continued

Corporate Objectives	Decision Criteria and Metrics	Definition	Metrics (Objective or Subjective Criteria)
Increase Sales	Market Share	Percent of total market held by the company	Objective
	Market Opportunity	Assessment of new market opportunities	Subjective
	Sales Growth	Assessment of ability to attract new customers	Subjective
Enhance Information Technology Performance	System Reliability	Percent uptime of the computer system interfaces	Objective
	System Interfaces	Ability to interface successfully with external systems and file submittal requirements	Subjective
	Flexibility	Assessment of the flexibility of the systems to adapt with new customers	Subjective

You need to ensure that the decision criteria can be supported by metrics that can be evaluated. The data for the metrics should be relatively easy to gather, maintain, and track on an ongoing basis. This provides the means to measure corporate performance against objectives important to the company.

8.4 Explore the Environment

8.4.1 Integrated Corporate Planning

In this section, you analyze the interactions and interdependencies between the various corporate areas. This can form a framework for zeroing in on the problems areas that need to be improved.

8.4.1.1 Assess the Scope of the Problem

The first step of the process is to identify the functional areas that should be included in the analysis. Not all areas have direct impact, but the related areas should be included in the assessment. From the established corporate objectives, it appears that you should include five areas.

- Customer Management
- Finance
- Information Technology
- Logistics
- Sales

8.4.1.2 Develop the Activity Relationship Matrix

For the five corporate areas, the activity matrix has been set up and is shown in Table 8.5. Tables 8.6 and 8.7 are used to represent the closeness scale and the reason for the closeness value. You need to capture the interactions between those related functional areas in the process. For example, the interactions or closeness rating between the functional area of Finance and Logistics have been rated as an A, Absolutely Necessary. These two functional areas must be in sync when decisions are made so that they can work together to achieve joint improvement

Table 8.5 Activity Relationship Matrix

From					
Department Listing	1	2	3	4	5
1. Customer Management		C	C	B	B
2. Finance			C	A	B
				1	
3. Information Technology				A	C
				1	
4. Logistics					B
5. Sales					

Table 8.6 Closeness Rating Scale

Value	Closeness	Line Code
A	Absolutely Necessary	▬▬▬
B	Very Important	▬▬
C	Important	───
D	Unimportant	
E	Undesirable	XXXX

Table 8.7 Reasons for Closeness Value

Reason for the Closeness Value	
Code	**Reason**
1	Interrelated Processes
2	Shared Resources
3	Same Management Chain

From the relationships you can see that Finance, Information Technology, and Logistics are closely related.

8.4.1.3 Quantify Performance with Industry Benchmarks and Performance Evaluations

The decision criteria are evaluated against the industry benchmarks and performance in the functional area. Table 8.8 shows the decision criteria and the results of that assessment.

Table 8.8 Industry Benchmark and Performance Evaluations

Performance Assessment from Corporate Priorities			
	Area	Benchmark Performance (1 high–5 low)	Aggregated Benchmark Performance (1 high–5 low)
1. Customer Management	Customer Calls	2	2.33
	Customer Turnover	3	
	Customer Satisfaction	2	

continues

Table 8.8 Industry Benchmark and Performance Evaluations, continued

Performance Assessment from Corporate Priorities

	Area	Benchmark Performance (1 high–5 low)	Aggregated Benchmark Performance (1 high–5 low)
2. Finance	Warehousing Cost per Unit	4	3.67
	Transportation Cost per Unit	3	
	Inventory Investment	4	
3. Information Technology	System Reliability	2	2.67
	System Interfaces	3	
	Flexibility	3	
4. Logistics	Warehouse Cycle Time	4	3.67
	On-Time Performance	3	
	Inventory Turnover	4	
5. Sales	Market Share	2	2.33
	Market Opportunity	3	
	Sales Growth	2	

You can see that two key areas stand out as being below acceptable performance as indicated by the industry benchmark performance, which are Finance and Logistics. The Activity Relationship Diagram in the next section documents these relationships and performance characteristics.

8.4.1.4 Develop the Activity Relationship Diagram

The activity relationship diagram is developed to account for the functional interactions along with the magnitude of the issues assessed against the industry benchmarks. Figure 8.1 shows the Activity Relationship Diagram with two different subsets of problem areas that are to be pursued. These include a subset of Logistics, Finance, and Information Technology and a subset of Finance, Logistics, and Sales. Further investigation is necessary to determine which high-impact areas to pursue to achieve the goals of the company.

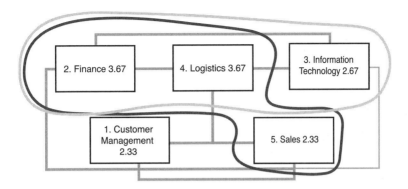

Figure 8.1 Activity Relationship Diagram for logistics provider

The diagram is constructed so that the areas with the greatest need for improvement and the closeness of the functions are shown at the top of the diagram. This creates a visual representation of the areas in which management can focus the improvement efforts. You also need to represent the closeness of the relationships so that the interactions between functions are captured in process enhancements. Then use corporate knowledge to identify specific improvement opportunities.

8.4.1.5 Determine the Variability of the Metrics and Financial Contribution of the Individual Functions

After key opportunity areas have been identified, further analysis is performed to pinpoint specific areas of opportunity. The variability associated with the benchmark assessments and the percent of the total budget that each area expends is identified and analyzed. Table 8.9 shows these relationships.

The additional data confirms that you need to further evaluate Logistics and Finance. Information Technology has a higher budget and greater variability, so it should also be included as a part of the improvement focus areas.

Table 8.9 Activity Relationship Diagram with Performance, Variability, and Budget Assessments

From

Department Listing	1	2	3	4	5	Aggregated Benchmark Performance (1 high–5 low)	Variability– Fuzzy or Statistical	Percent of Total Budget
1. Customer Management		C	C	B	B	2.33	Low	10%
2. Finance			C	A 1	B	3.67	Medium	30%
3. Information Technology				A 1	C	2.67	Medium	20%
4. Logistics					B	3.67	High	30%
5. Sales						2.33	Medium	10%

8.4.1.6 Identify Specific Problem Areas to Improve

Because the focus areas are Logistics, Finance, and Information Technology, specific problems are identified within these three areas. The performance assessment based on corporate priorities and the cross-functional relationship assessments helps to avoid taking a stove-piped approach to problem solving. In this case, supply chain activities, the systems that support these activities, and the financial implications of inventory investment and cycle times all contribute to overall corporate performance. Use specific performance metrics to identify opportunity areas such as warehousing costs, inventory investment, cycle times, inventory turnover, and system interfaces and flexibility. Some high potential cross-functional areas for focus are listed here.

- Material flow through the system
- Inventory levels and inventory investment at each point of the supply chain
- System interfaces enabling the processing of material through the supply chain
- Forecast accuracy for purchased and manufacturing parts

The focus areas identified all have a common thread. Performance in each of these areas is driven by the efficient physical and systematic movement of product through the supply chain. To assist in pinpointing specific areas of improvement, the key supply chain processes and associated metrics will be represented in a business process model.

8.5 Explore the Scope of the Problem and Its Importance

Figure 8.2 shows a grouping of Logistics, Finance, and Information Technology and Logistics, Finance, and Sales have been identified as key focus areas that you can investigate to improve operational and financial performance. These three areas have strong functional relationships and have lower functional performance levels as determined from the benchmarking and variability analysis. Most likely, cross functional improvements can have a positive impact on all three of the areas.

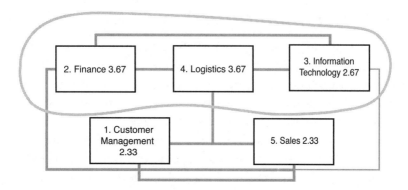

Figure 8.2 Activity Relationship diagram with cross-functional focus areas

8.5.1 Identification of the Problem Areas

The executive team has chosen to focus improvements in the integrated areas of Logistics, Finance, and Information Technology

The metrics and variability associated with the processes and the percent of the total budget for these areas are shown in Table 8.10.

In aggregate, these three functional areas account for 80 percent of the total budget. Certain performance metrics such as warehousing cost per unit, inventory turnover, system interfaces and flexibility, inventory investment, and warehouse cycle times are the lower performing metrics associated with the functional areas. The variability associated with the processes is high in each of the functional areas as well. We have identified the problem focus and scope and ensure we can improve performance and improve productivity.

A number of areas can be pursued for improvement. These include improving the material flow through the system to improve cycle times and inventory investments, monitoring of the supply chain on a proactive basis to identify bottlenecks, and accumulation of points, improving system interfaces to decrease the turn-around time of procurement and ordering activities, and improving forecast accuracies. Functional executives typically have their own performance measures based on key metrics associated with their areas and global corporate metrics. Because of relationships between different corporate functions, collaboration between different functional area executives in the pursuit of improvements should have benefits across a number of related areas.

Table 8.10 Performance Evaluation of Cross-Functional Focus Areas

Area		Benchmark Performance (1 high–5 low)	Aggregated Benchmark Performance (1 high–5 low)	Variability– Fuzzy or Statistical	Percent of Total Budget
Finance	Warehousing Cost per Unit	4	3.67	Medium	30%
	Transportation Cost per Unit	3			
	Inventory Investment	4			
Information Technology	System Reliability	2	2.67	Medium	20%
	System Interfaces	3			
	Flexibility	3			
Logistics	Warehouse Cycle Time	4	3.67	High	30%
	On-Time Performance	3			
	Inventory Turnover	4			

Because this is a supply chain system, gaining a clear understanding of the integrated processes is important. The executive team feels that there is significant opportunity to improve these integrated systems; therefore, they want to focus on developing an integrated computer system that reports the inventory levels, operating costs, and cycle times of each of the main processes. This should require minimal data to be stored in a database and making this information available corporate wide. This can also provide a framework for ongoing evaluation of the current state and future improvements and can also identify key areas in which performance can be enhanced.

8.5.2 Definition of the Sphere of Control

Key activities that impact the supply chain are identified; activities such as acquisition, receiving, warehousing, and transportation are included in the analysis, the system interfaces that support these processes, and the dollar investments associated with them. Additionally, other functional areas such as sales, forecasting, order entry, returns, and so on are important to the overall success of the operations in these areas. These activities will be included as part of the sphere of control in this study.

8.5.3 Identification of the Key Activities, Processes, Systems, and Influences

Specific areas such as warehousing costs, inventory investment, inventory turnover, and system interfaces have been identified as areas targeted for improvement. It is necessary to identify high-level processes and external influences that impact performance in these key areas. A high-level business process model is developed to capture these influences and understand their interactions. Key, high-level activities are identified for each of the functional areas as they relate to the overall corporate processes. Figure 8.3 shows these activities, processes, systems, and influences.

The intent of the high-level business process model is to identify the key upstream and downstream impacts surrounding an identified opportunity area. In this case, functions such as sales, finance, systems, logistics, and repair functions all interact with the flow of material through the supply chain. Each of these areas of high-level activities can be decomposed into lower-level processes to identify specific opportunity areas.

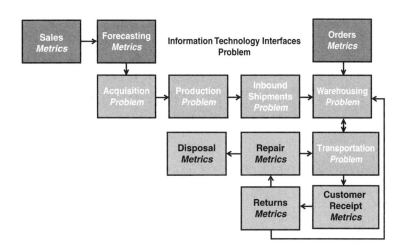

Figure 8.3 High-level business process model for focused improvement areas

8.5.4 Upstream and Downstream Interactions

The upstream and downstream interactions are included in the exploration of the problem scope and the development of the high-level business process model. Upstream areas include sales, forecasting, and ordering processes. Downstream areas include customer receipt, returns, repair, and disposal activities. Together, these upstream, downstream, and identified problem areas constitute the operating environment that will be investigated with the model for improvement opportunities.

8.5.5 Identification of the Data That Supports the Measurement of the Objectives

Use benchmark data for each of the functional areas to measure the effect of the improvements on the various performance areas. You can gather additional data and metrics for volumes, cycle times, and inventory investment to measure at each point in the supply chain. Additional metrics may include the following:

- Forecast accuracy
- Order data and trends
- Percent returns and repairs

The data identified here will be further analyzed to identify specific areas to focus individual improvement efforts.

8.6 Data Mining and Statistical Analysis

From the business modeling effort, the data used to support the analysis is then gathered. In reviewing the model you need to first understand the metrics associated with the problem areas identified and then relate the potential upstream impacts and downstream effects to the problem area metrics and include them in the model.

Data exists to measure the volumes, cycle times, and inventory investment at each of the key areas of the logistics supply chain, which includes Acquisition, Production, Inbound Shipments, Warehousing, and Transportation. Initially, gather this information by month to determine the overall operating characteristics associated with the process. Table 8.11 shows averages by month for each of the identified metrics.

This data is a starting point to quantify the logistics and investment performance levels in each of the subsections of the supply chain. Each of the subsections of the supply chain is comprised of overall steps and processes. Attempting to analyze each individual component of the pipeline initially may cause you to lose sight of the overall picture and opportunity areas to pursue. Because of this, the supply chain is grouped into subsections and data is gathered to quantify the performance for the subsection.

Certain sections of the pipeline (such as acquisition and production) show long lead times from the time that the request is made to the time that product is actually shipped to the warehouse. Simple statistics are run on the data to determine the mean and variability associated with the performance, as shown in Table 8.12.

Determining the average and standard deviation associated with the monthly numbers provides aggregate information to determine areas to further study. Areas with long cycle times and high variability along with significant inventory investment highlight opportunity areas. By using simple graphs, you can determine any potential anomalies and cyclical effects seen throughout the year. This is noted in Figure 8.4.

In this case, cyclical patterns exist throughout the year, which can provide insights into potential problem areas.

Additionally, you need to determine similar high-level performance metrics in upstream areas and areas impacted by the effects of the issues. Key in the initial data analysis is to gain information that can point to potential areas for improvement.

8.7 Solve the Problem and Measure the Results

The logistics pipeline moves a large amount of product and contains a significant level of inventory investment. The successful operation of the inventory pipeline requires that each of the individual components of the pipeline operate well. Because the individual components and parts make up the pipeline as a whole, you need to measure and monitor performance on an ongoing basis. Because of these operating parameters, the decision was made to develop an automated model of pipeline operations to monitor activities and to target performance improvements on an ongoing basis. To do this, you must determine the structure, capabilities, and types of information that need to be captured in the monitoring system. Figure 8.5 shows an enhanced view of the pipeline subcomponents and the type of data that will be monitored within the system. The monitoring includes both the physical movement of product along with the system processing steps so that you can assess both the physical and the system performance.

Table 8.11 Key Metrics by Month

	January	February	March	April	May
Acquisition					
Cycle Time (average days)	140	125	140	147	178
Volume (total parts)	162,224	152,343	161,691	126,116	107,821
Inventory Investment ($)	$ 3,497,387	$ 2,616,188	$ 2,786,605	$ 2,734,130	$ 3,421,143
Production					
Cycle Time (average days)	89	80	145	150	80
Volume (total parts)	223,509	200,865	165,370	218,936	208,860
Inventory Investment ($)	$ 3,797,884	$ 3,293,041	$ 3,416,084	$ 4,278,248	$ 4,450,973
Inbound Shipments					
Cycle Time (average days)	22	14	17	10	5
Volume (total parts)	190,426	211,550	247,852	163,634	244,779
Inventory Investment ($)	$ 3,792,128	$ 3,902,744	$ 3,755,293	$ 3,037,536	$ 3,148,329
Warehouse					
Cycle Time (average days)	2	1	3	1	1
Volume (total parts)	289,940	238,429	164,270	272,700	234,748
Inventory Investment ($)	$ 15,364,062	$ 13,734,733	$ 17,407,482	$ 13,677,343	$ 17,732,607
Transportation					
Cycle Time (average days)	2	4	2	4	4
Volume (total parts)	190,194	253,728	286,105	152,225	299,568
Inventory Investment ($)	$ 3,644,115	$ 3,675,756	$ 3,860,213	$ 3,493,015	$ 3,035,614
Logistics Pipeline Total					
Cycle Time (average days)	255	224	307	312	268
Volume (total parts)	1,056,293	1,056,915	1,025,288	933,611	1,095,776
Inventory Investment ($)	$ 30,095,576	$ 27,222,462	$ 31,225,677	$ 27,220,272	$ 31,788,666

June	July	August	September	October	November	December
168	156	146	160	157	153	165
197,454	121,625	137,343	156,155	120,489	125,598	151,922
$ 2,613,701	$ 3,436,990	$ 3,333,798	$ 2,918,680	$ 2,788,250	$ 3,150,360	$ 2,604,419
77	69	107	101	136	119	73
215,849	222,694	163,422	179,617	233,069	232,456	175,123
$ 3,288,500	$ 3,117,384	$ 3,069,827	$ 4,170,138	$ 4,409,108	$ 3,176,129	$ 3,332,665
17	10	6	6	15	5	6
212,611	215,567	201,583	206,742	193,393	161,693	217,948
$ 3,824,953	$ 4,304,572	$ 3,610,980	$ 3,630,952	$ 3,619,314	$ 3,081,980	$ 4,192,816
2	3	2	2	3	3	1
290,055	246,783	169,152	215,047	285,609	171,810	267,727
$ 10,761,764	$ 13,209,011	$ 15,865,271	$ 16,563,653	$ 17,619,572	$ 15,293,373	$ 17,205,297
3	2	2	2	2	4	3
299,216	292,950	196,676	164,503	150,884	289,964	152,217
$ 3,412,846	$ 4,497,952	$ 3,562,163	$ 4,039,983	$ 3,236,053	$ 4,138,028	$ 3,535,526
267	240	263	271	313	284	248
1,215,185	1,099,619	868,176	922,064	983,444	981,521	964,937
$ 23,901,764	$ 28,565,909	$ 29,442,039	$ 31,323,406	$ 31,672,297	$ 28,839,870	$ 30,870,723

Table 8.12 Logistics Pipeline Statistics

	Average	Standard Deviation
Acquisition		
Cycle Time (average days)	141	48.1
Volume (total parts)	130,992	46,309
Inventory Investment ($)	$ 2,687,874	$ 922,818
Production		
Cycle Time (average days)	90	31.9
Volume (total parts)	183,487	64,396
Inventory Investment ($)	$ 3,194,445	$ 1,104,006
Inbound Shipments		
Cycle Time (average days)	9	4.5
Volume (total parts)	182,413	60,851
Inventory Investment ($)	$ 3,369,843	$ 1,167,573
Warehouse		
Cycle Time (average days)	2	0.8
Volume (total parts)	214,553	76,558
Inventory Investment ($)	$ 13,782,960	$ 4,845,976
Transportation		
Cycle Time (average days)	2	0.9
Volume (total parts)	204,282	80,165
Inventory Investment ($)	$ 3,389,353	$ 1,187,614
Logistics Pipeline Total		
Cycle Time (average days)	243	83.0
Volume (total parts)	905,176	320,232
Inventory Investment ($)	$ 26,258,122	$ 9,250,714

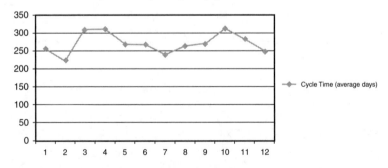

Figure 8.4 Yearly logistics pipeline cycle times

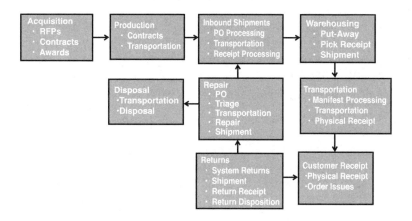

Figure 8.5 Fundamental components of the logistics pipeline monitoring system

Track data at the subcomponent level and then aggregate to the pipeline component and total logistics pipeline. Track performance metrics including the following:

- Cycle time
- Volume
- Investment value

The pipeline analyzer maintains the parts' level data, which is categorized into the following.

- Company
- System
- Part number
- Part group
- Sources
- Priority
- Review period (month, quarter, and so on)

Additionally, analysis can be done with the system that includes

- Compare Analysis
- Trend Analysis
- Variability Analysis
- What-If Analysis

Figures 8.6 through 8.8 show an example of a developed logistics pipeline system. Data for each segment of the pipeline was captured and stored in the database system. The users viewed processing time and investment value at each of the sub segments of the pipeline and for the component parts. Forecasts were generated and actual performance was tracked. Users performed comparative and what-if analysis for the parts and systems on an ongoing basis. This provided a view of areas of opportunity for improvement and performance tracking. Figure 8.6 provides a visual of the subcomponents of the primary sections of the pipeline.

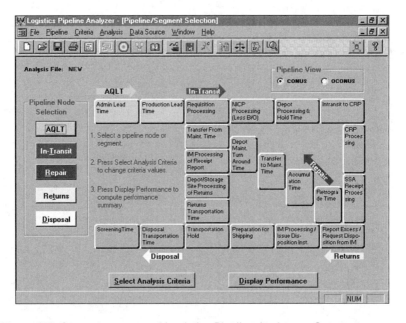

Figure 8.6 Computer screen of Logistics Pipeline Analyzer – Segment Selection

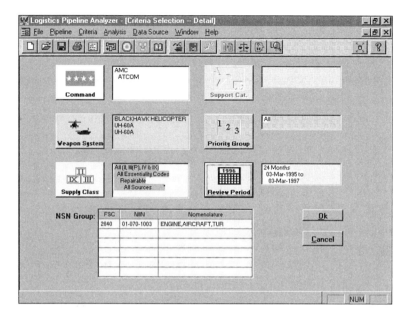

Figure 8.7 Computer screen of Logistics Pipeline Analyzer – Analysis Criteria Selection

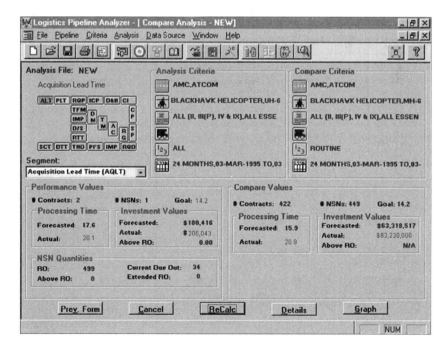

Figure 8.8 Computer screen of Logistics Pipeline Analyzer – Performance Evaluation

Users varied the granularity of their analyses by selecting different criteria. You can view the performance of the entire supply chain for a system and individual component parts, as well.

Performance data is provided based on the criteria and analysis as selected by the user. The user can monitor the specific performance metrics for the logistics pipeline and identify areas of opportunity that develop.

8.8 Evaluate the Results and Do Sensitivity Analysis

The system was implemented to monitor cycle times, volume, and investment value at each stage of the pipeline. The objective of the system is to monitor and assess key performance characteristics associated with the logistics pipeline. Each of the pipeline segments can be impacted by Operational Performance and System Performance issues, as shown in Table 8.13.

Table 8.13 Performance Evaluation Characteristics

Pipeline Segment	Operational Performance	System Performance
Acquisition		
RFPs	X	
Contracts	X	
Awards	X	
Production		
Contracts	X	X
Production	X	
Inbound Shipments		
PO Processing		X
Transportation	X	X
Receipt Processing	X	X
Warehousing		
Put-Away	X	X
Pick Receipt	X	X

continues

Table 8.13 Performance Evaluation Characteristics, continued

Pipeline Segment	Operational Performance	System Performance
Shipment	X	X
Disposal		
Transportation	X	X
Disposal	X	
Repair		
PO	X	X
Triage	X	
Transportation	X	X
Repair	X	
Shipment	X	X
Transportation		
Manifest Processing	X	X
Transportation	X	
Physical Receipt	X	X
Returns		
System Returns	X	X
Shipment	X	X
Return Receipt	X	X
Return Disposition	X	
Customer Receipt		
Physical Receipt	X	X
Order Issues	X	X

You can relate improvements in many of the performance areas to the benchmark criteria used to evaluate the functional performance areas. Assessing the performance in each of the pipeline segments and sub segments and linking these pipeline segment performance areas to specific benchmark performance criteria can lead to the identification of improvement opportunities. This analysis was conducted and a number of improvement opportunities have been identified.

- Improve system response times in P.O. processing, receipt processing, pick receipt, and manifest processing to reduce cycle time and inventory investment.

- Improve the operational performance in the Acquisition pipeline to reduce the overall lead time and investment allocation.
- Implement a transportation optimization program to reduce transportation costs.
- Improve repair processing to reduce costs and improve quality of product.

Each of these opportunities was evaluated using the key benchmark criteria, development cost, and economic benefit to determine which course of action should be initially taken.

An economic analysis is performed for each of the identified alternatives. The cost breakdown structure and life cycle costs described in Section 6.4 form the foundation for evaluating each of the alternatives to determine their economic benefit. Applicable costs for each of the alternatives are identified over the multiyear time horizon. These individual costs are rolled up into the four major cost categories: Research and Development, Investment, Operations and Maintenance, and System Phase-Out/Disposal. Table 8.14 shows the economic evaluation of these alternatives.

The cost and revenue streams are used to compute the present value of the alternatives identified as problem solutions. This economic benefit or present value of the alternatives becomes part of the decision matrix used to evaluate the alternatives.

The decision matrix in Table 8.15 shows these evaluations where the Simple Additive Weights Method was used to prioritize these alternatives. From the evaluation, it appears that improving the system response times would be the best course of action that contributes the most to achieving the operational objectives.

Table 8.14 Economic Evaluation of Alternatives

| | | Cost Breakdown | | | | | | |
		Research and Development	Investment	Operations and Maintenance	System Phase-Out and Disposal	Total Cost	Revenue or Savings Benefit	Present Value of Alternative
Improve System Response Times	Year 0	$1,000,000	$1,000,000			$ 2,000,000	$ -	$1,497,942
	Year 1		$3,000,000	$1,000,000		$ 4,000,000	$ 5,000,000	
	Year 2			$1,500,000	$500,000	$ 2,000,000	$5,000,000	
Improve Acquisi-tion Lead Time Performance	Year 0	$250,000	$500,000			$750,000	$ -	$ 784,636
	Year 1		$500,000			$500,000	$1,000,000	
	Year 2			$250,000		$250,000	$1,500,000	
Reduce Transportation Costs	Year 0		$500,000			$500,000	$ -	$4,352,538
	Year 1		$750,000	$250,000		$1,000,000	$3,000,000	
	Year 2			$500,000		$500,000	$4,000,000	
Improve Repair Processes	Year 0	$ 1,000,000	$1,000,000			$2,000,000	$ -	$1,429,355
	Year 1	$3,000,000		$2,000,000		$5,000,000	$5,000,000	
	Year 2			$500,000	$500,000	$1,000,000	$5,000,000	

Table 8.15 Ranking of Alternatives

| | | 10% | 10% | 25% | 20% | 15% | 20% | 10% | |
| | | | | | Importance Weight | | | | |
Alternatives	Development Cost	Development Cost (Scale)	Inventory Investment Improvement (Scale: 1 (low)–5 (high))	System Interface Improvement Scale: 1 (low)–5 (high)	Transportation Cost Improvement (Scale: 1 (low)–5 (high))	Warehouse Cycle Time Improvement (Scale: 1 (low)–5 (high))	Economic Benefit (Scale: 1 (low)–5 (high))	Score
1. Improve System Response Times	$8,000,000	1	3	5	2	3	3	3.05
2. Improve Acquisition Lead Time Performance	$1,500,000	3	3	3	2	1	2	2.35
3. Reduce Transportation Costs	$2,000,000	3	2	1	5	2	4	2.55
4. Improve Repair Processes	$8,000,000	5	2	1	2	3	3	2.4

continues

Table 8.15   Ranking of Alternatives, continued

Development Cost Scale
5: Very low <$500K
4: Low >=$500K to <$1M
3: Medium >=$1M to <$2.5M
2: High >=$2.5M to <$5M
1: Very high >=$5M

Economic Benefit Scale
1: Very low <$500K
2: Low >=$500K to <$1M
3: Medium >=$1M to <$2.5M
4: High >= $2.5M to <$5M
5: Very high >=$5M

Additional analyses can be done to determine other what-if scenarios and sensitivity analyses. Seeing that the alternatives are fairly close in scoring, you can test certain criteria to determine if changes in the evaluation score lead to the selection of a different alternative to pursue. Table 8.16 shows that if the scores for the decision criteria Inventory Investment Improvement and System Interface Improvement increase for Alternative 2, then Improve Acquisition Lead Time Performance will make both Alternative 1 and Alternative 2 equally desirable to pursue.

If the acquisition lead time improvement project was structured so it had a greater impact on inventory investment and the improvement to system interfaces, this project would be equally as beneficial to improve the system response times. You can use these types of sensitivity analyses to quickly explore any number of scenarios as changes occur.

Table 8.16 Sensitivity Analysis of Alternatives

| | | | Importance Weight | | | | | |
| | | 10% | 25% | 20% | 15% | 20% | 10% | |
Alternatives	Development Cost	Development Cost (Scale)	Inventory Investment Improvement (Scale: 1 (low)–5 (high))	System Interface Improvement (Scale: 1 (low)–5 (high))	Transportation Cost Improvement (Scale: 1 (low)–5 (high))	Warehouse Cycle Time Improvement (Scale: 1 (low)–5 (high))	Economic Benefit (Scale: 1 (low)–5 (high))	Score
1. Improve System Response Times	$8,000,000	1	3	5	2	3	3	3.05
2. Improve Acquisition Lead Time Performance	$1,500,000	3	5	4	2	1	2	3.05
3. Reduce Transportation Costs	$2,000,000	3	2	1	5	2	4	2.55
4. Improve Repair Processes	$8,000,000	5	2	1	2	3	3	2.4

8.9 Summary

This case study provides an analysis of a logistics service provider owned by a parent company. The logistics company functions as an independent entity from the parent company; however, it must support the parent company logistics requirements and provide services to outside organizations. The logistics pipeline of related activities is complicated with warehouse cycle time considerations, system interfaces, inventory investment, and transportation costs that must be considered to determine areas to improve in the company to make it more competitive with other companies in the industry. Because of this, it is necessary to track and monitor the various activities throughout the supply chain to identify opportunity areas and enhancements that can drive performance improvements. After improvements are identified, the economic value associated with the improvement is analyzed so that the company can most efficiently utilize its resources to improve operations.

9

New Product Development

9.1 Introduction

This chapter demonstrates the process for selecting new products to develop within your company. A step-by-step review of the problem demonstrates the methods used in this book to select new products.

In this scenario, an emerging company wants to optimize the products that it brings to the market place. This company is approximately 10 years old and has grown quickly has the capability to quickly innovate and bring new products to the market place. Because of the company's growth from a more entrepreneurial company to a maturing, established company, many of its processes are not structured.

The company hopes to continue its growth but has limited resources. At this point, management needs to ensure that the products brought to market meet the growth objectives of the company. The time has passed where new products can be tested and mistakes easily absorbed and not hurt the company's finances. Because of this, it needs to restructure the new product development processes ensuring the greatest possibility of success.

9.2 Define the Objectives

Company executives conducted strategic planning sessions to formalize their view of the future direction of the company. Through these sessions, the executives agreed that they would like to keep the entrepreneurial philosophy in the company but would like to develop a structured process that ensures the product line meets the goals and objectives of the company.

Key in this approach is establishing the strategic objectives. Through a number of discussions, they arrived at the following high-level objectives:

- **Enhance market position**—The goal is to engage in development and commercialization efforts that position the company as proficient suppliers within the industry and develop a leadership position.

- **Maximize profit**—Executives want to ensure that the products they pursue provide a significant long-term financial benefit to the company.

- **Maximize resource utilization**—The executives want to minimize the need for new plants and facilities and develop products consistent with the current core competencies and aligned with the current markets.

- **Maximize the probability of success**—Although the executives will take risks with new product development efforts, they want to pursue those products that have the highest chance of being successful.

- **Strategic alignment**—The executives also want to develop products that complement the current business activities and identify barriers that may cause issues in launching a new product.

From the sessions, the executives felt that they have established the cross-functional objectives of the company.

9.3 Developing Decision Criteria and Metrics

By following the process steps, the decision criteria and metrics are developed for the company.

9.3.1 Step 1: Establish Overall Objectives and Goals

The objectives developed by the executive group are then used to develop metrics that measure the success of the company's product development activities. These objectives and goals are to:

- Enhance market position.
- Maximize profit.
- Maximize resource utilization.
- Maximize the probability of success.
- Strategic alignment.

9.3.2 Step 2: Weight the Objectives to Determine Their Importance

Group decision-making techniques are used to develop importance weighting by the executive group. Each executive is asked to assign a percentage of importance for each of the five objectives. Table 9.1 shows the results.

Table 9.1 Corporate Objectives and Weights

Corporate Objectives	#1 Objective Weights	#2 Objective Weights	#3 Objective Weights	#4 Objective Weights	#5 Objective Weights	Overall Objective Weights
Enhance Market Position	30%	20%	20%	20%	25%	23%
Maximize Profit	30%	25%	40%	20%	25%	28%
Maximize Resource Utilization	10%	15%	15%	30%	15%	17%
Maximize the Probability of Success	10%	15%	15%	20%	20%	16%
Strategic Alignment	20%	25%	10%	10%	15%	16%

continues

The exercise shows that holistically, all the executives believe that enhancing the market position and maximizing profit are the two most important objectives. The other three objectives of maximizing resource utilization, maximizing the probability of success, and strategic alignment are of lesser importance. This information is used in the decision process to determine which products should be pursued.

9.3.3 Step 3: Select the Decision Criteria

Each of the objectives has a number of decision criteria that you can use to measure the success of achieving the agreed-upon objectives. Industry benchmark criteria are beneficial in the development of these decision criteria for assessing the success of the new products, which are communicated to management. Based on an understanding of the problems to be solved, the decision criteria in Table 9.2 have been established for each of the objectives.

Table 9.2 Decision Criteria and Metrics

Corporate Objectives	Overall Objective Weights	Decision Criteria and Metrics
Enhance Market Position	23%	Ability to Market
		New/Existing Market
		Market Attractiveness
		Market Size of Potential
		Market Growth Potential
		Number of Potential Customers
		Profitability of Customers
		Customer Satisfaction with Current Products
Maximize Profit	28%	After Tax Margin/ROI
		Payback Period
		Net Present Value

continues

Table 9.2 Decision Criteria and Metrics, continued

Corporate Objectives	Overall Objective Weights	Decision Criteria and Metrics
Maximize Resource Utilization	17%	Technical Development Requirements
		Market Resource Requirements
		Fits our Production Processes/ Equipment
		Build to Advantage on One or More Strengths
Maximize the Probability of Success	16%	Probability of Technical Success
		Probability of Commercial Success
Strategic Alignment	16%	Strategic Alignment
		Size of Competitive Barriers
		Sustainability of Barriers
		Competitors Attacked
		Intensity of Competition
		Opportunity to Obtain Price Premium
		Product Advantage to Customer Versus Competition

9.3.4 Step 4: Weight the Criteria to Determine Their Importance

The executive group then weight the decision criteria to determine the importance of each (see Table 9.3). This again provides focus to the actual problem areas that should be targeted for improvement.

Develop Decision Criteria Metrics

Each of the metrics identified are then defined so that they can be used in the performance assessment of each of the objectives. In this case, most of the decision criteria are industry benchmarks. You can use other subjective decision criteria based on expert opinion and industry knowledge. Table 9.4 shows the decision criteria from industry benchmark/objective data or subjective analysis.

Table 9.3 Decision Criteria Weighting

Corporate Objectives	Overall Objective Weights	Decision Criteria and Metrics	Decision Criteria Weight	Resulting Criteria Weight
Enhance Market Position	23%	Ability to Market	5%	1%
		New/Existing Market	5%	1%
		Market Attractiveness	10%	2%
		Market Size of Potential	20%	5%
		Market Growth Potential	20%	5%
		Number of Potential Customers	20%	5%
		Profitability of Customers	10%	2%
		Customer Satisfaction with Current Products	10%	2%
Maximize Profit	28%	After Tax Margin/ROI	40%	11%
		Payback Period	25%	7%
		Net Present Value	35%	10%
Maximize Resource Utilization	17%	Technical Development Requirements	25%	4%
		Market Resource Requirements	20%	3%
		Fits our Production Processes/Equipment	30%	5%
		Build to Advantage on One or More Strengths	25%	4%
Maximize the Probability of Success	16%	Probability of Technical Success	50%	8%
		Probability of Commercial Success	50%	8%

continues

Table 9.3 Decision Criteria Weighting, continued

Corporate Objectives	Overall Objective Weights	Decision Criteria and Metrics	Decision Criteria Weight	Resulting Criteria Weight
Strategic Alignment	16%	Strategic Alignment	25%	4%
		Size of Competitive Barriers	20%	3%
		Sustainability of Barriers	15%	2%
		Competitors Attacked	10%	2%
		Intensity of Competition	10%	2%
		Opportunity to Obtain Price Premium	10%	2%
		Product Advantage to Customer Versus Competition	10%	2%

Table 9.4 Decision Criteria and Metrics Definitions

Corporate Objectives	Decision Criteria and Metrics	Definition	Objective or Subjective
Enhance Market Position	Ability to Market	The ability to identify and reach the key purchaser influencer	Subjective
	New/Existing Market	The amount of effort required to build the market	Subjective
	Market Attractiveness	Attractive markets are sizable, profitable, growing with competitive advantage	Subjective
	Market Size of Potential	Maximum of attainable sales in the third year of commercial operations	Subjective
	Market Growth Potential	Rate of growth for only the portion of the market that can be reasonably captured	Subjective
	Number of Potential Customers	Number of potential customers who will be interested in the proposed offering	Subjective
	Profitability of Customers	Customers likely to desire value added offerings vs. price compare	Subjective
	Customer Satisfaction with Current Products	Customers well satisfied with current offerings and less likely to accept substitutes	Objective
Maximize Profit	After Tax Margin/ROI	After Tax Return on Investment	Objective
	Payback Period	Number of years to pay back product investment	Objective
	Net Present Value	Discounted cash flow of revenue and expense money streams	Objective

continues

Corporate Objectives	Decision Criteria and Metrics	Definition	Objective or Subjective
Maximize Resource Utilization	Technical Development Requirements	Level of new technical effort required for the product development	Subjective
	Market Resource Requirements	Level of investment of resources required to achieve market presence	Subjective
	Fits our Production Processes/ Equipment	Projects that build out on facilities alread in place	Subjective
	Build to Advantage on One or More Strengths	Builds on a current strength	Subjective
Maximize the Probability of Success	Probability of Technical Success	Probabality that the product will be technically successful	Subjective
	Probability of Commercial Success	Probability that the product will be commercially successful	Subjective
Strategic Alignment	Strategic Alignment	The ability for the initiative to provide value added offerings	Subjective
	Size of Competitive Barriers	Ability to prevent competition from copying products	Subjective
	Sustainability of Barriers	The time in which the competitive barrier can be sustained	Subjective
	Competitors Attacked	The ability to tie up key competitors in the offering	Subjective
	Intensity of Competition	Number of competitors jockeying for position with no clear leader	Subjective
	Opportunity to Obtain Price Premium	Ability to differentiate our product and get a price premium	Subjective
	Product Advantage to Customer Versus Competition	The amount of product advantage the program will create versus a competitive offering	Subjective

You need to ensure that the decision criteria metrics can be supported by data. The metric data should be relatively easy to gather, maintain, and track on an ongoing basis. This provides the means to measure corporate success and meet company objectives.

9.4 Explore the Environment

You then need to explore the scope and relationship of the development of each new product to the current product line.

9.4.1 Integrated Corporate Planning

This section analyzes the interactions and interdependencies between the various organizational units. This forms a framework for zeroing in on the problem areas that must be included in the analysis to select new products.

9.4.1.1 Assess the Scope of the Problem

The first step of the process is to identify the functional areas that should be included in the analysis. Not all areas can have a direct impact, but you should include related areas in the assessment. From the established corporate objectives, following are five areas to include.

- Product development
- Strategy
- Marketing
- Finance
- Operations

9.4.1.2 Develop the Activity Relationship Matrix

Incorporating the five corporate areas, the activity matrix has been set up, as shown in Table 9.5. Capture the interactions between the various functions with this step in the process. For example, the interactions or closeness rating between the functional area of product development and strategy are rated as an A, Absolutely Necessary. These two functional areas must be in sync when decisions are made so that they can achieve joint goals.

Table 9.5 Activity Relationship Matrix

From					
Department Listing	**1**	**2**	**3**	**4**	**5**
1. Product Development		A	A	B	B
2. Strategy			A	B	C
3. Marketing				B	B
4. Finance					A
5. Operations					

For the five functions, you need to establish the closeness rating and the reasons for the closeness as shown in Table 9.6 and 9.7.

Table 9.6 Closeness Rating Scale

Value	Closeness	Line Code
A	Absolutely Necessary	═══════
B	Very Important	▬▬▬▬▬
C	Important	──────
D	Unimportant	
E	Undesirable	XXXX

Table 9.7 Reasons for Closeness Value

Code	Reason
1	Interrelated Processes
2	Shared Resources
3	Same Management Chain

9.4.1.3 Quantify Performance with Industry Benchmarks and Performance Evaluations

This company established a comprehensive set of decision criteria. The key decision criteria are used to benchmark the company against other companies in the industry to determine where it is doing well and where it needs to improve new products. Table 9.8 shows the decision criteria/industry benchmark assessment.

Table 9.8 Benchmark Performance Evaluation

	Area	Benchmark Performance (1 high– 5 low)	Aggregated Benchmark Performance (1 high– 5 low)
1. Product Development	Innovation	3	2.33
	Technological Success	2	
	Commercial Success	2	
2. Strategy	Strategic Alignment with Competencies	3	2.67
	Market/Technology Competitiveness	3	
	Growth	2	
3. Marketing	Market Share	2	2.33
	Competitive Barriers	3	
	Ability to Attract New Customers	2	
4. Finance	EBITA	3	3.33
	Free Cash Flow	4	
	After Tax Margin/ROI	3	
5. Operations	Technical Development Requirements	3	3.33
	Market Resource Requirements	4	
	Fits our Production Processes/Equipment	3	

You can see that two key areas stand out as being below industry benchmark performance: Finance and Operations. The next section documents these relationships and performance characteristics in the Activity Relationship Diagram.

9.4.1.4 Develop the Activity Relationship Diagram

The Activity Relationship Diagram accounts for the functional interactions assessed against the industry benchmarks, as shown in Figure 9.1.

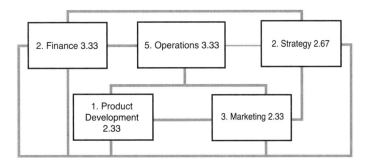

Figure 9.1 Activity Relationship Diagram

Figure 9.1 is constructed so that the areas with the greatest opportunity to introduce new products and the closeness of the functions are shown at the top of the diagram. This creates a visual representation of the areas in which management focuses the productivity improvement efforts. It is important to represent the closeness of the relationships so that the interactions between functions are captured in process enhancements. Corporate knowledge can then be used to identify specific problems when introducing a new product.

This diagram shows some differences from the other studies shown in the text. There are significant closeness relationships between a number of different areas including Strategy and Product Development, Product Development and Marketing, Finance and Operations, and Strategy and Marketing. These significant relationships lead to implied closeness relationships in other areas. Due to the young age of the company and its rapid growth, many of these functions have not been separated into the more stove-piped traditional functional relationships. This may have served the company well in its growth, but at this point, the process needs more structure and decisions are made that support the overall company objectives, which are highly interrelated. The variability and budget analysis identify additional performance improvement opportunities when introducing a new product.

9.4.1.5 Identify Specific Problem Areas to Improve

Interestingly enough, although some of the functional areas perform better than the industry benchmarks, such as Product Development and Marketing, the variability associated with their benchmark scores has been high, as shown in Table 9.9. This shows that the company has been successful; however, the processes are not in control for consistent performance results. This makes sense knowing that the company has grown quickly and performed well, but still is in need of structure of the processes.

The various functions are interrelated and have operated inconsistently at times. The new products developed by the company are its lifeblood. A potential area of focus is to standardize decisions and operational processes to improve the consistency of selecting products to introduce and have an integrated product development and evaluation process.

9.5 Explore the Scope of the Problem and Its Importance

The company needs a structured process for new product development so each new product is fairly compared using the same process for new products and old.

9.5.1 Identification of the Problem Areas

This analysis confirms the need to standardize processes across the organization. The functional areas are highly related, and the lifeblood of the company is new product development. The executive team has decided that their focus is to standardize the process for new product selection. This process can incorporate key evaluation criteria from all areas of the company so that an integrated selection process determines which products are best overall to bring to market.

Table 9.9 Activity Relationship Matrix with Performance Evaluation, Variability, and Percent of Total Budget

From

Department Listing	1	2	3	4	5	Aggregated Benchmark Performance (1 high–5 low)	Variability–Fuzzy or Statistical	Percent of Total Budget
1. Product Development		A	A	B	B	2.33	High	25%
2. Strategy			A	B	C	2.67	Medium	10%
3. Marketing				B	B	2.33	High	25%
4. Finance					A	3.33	Medium	20%
5. Operations						3.33	Medium	20%

Because the specific problem area has been identified, you can document the current business process and enhance that process to provide a standardized approach to companywide product development selections.

9.5.2 Definition of the Sphere of Control

Figure 9.2 shows the business process diagram for the current process for the New Product Development selection process in most companies. Each of the different groups in the organization submits ideas for funding approval, and funds are allocated to the various ideas and products based on availability. The new product ideas are funded based on the ability of the various internal organizations to convince the budgeting group of their merit. There is minimal rigor surrounding the evaluation and selection process currently used. Those ideas that sound best are funded, or those individuals that can generate the most compelling arguments are provided the resources for development. These requests are made on an ad hoc basis at unspecified intervals.

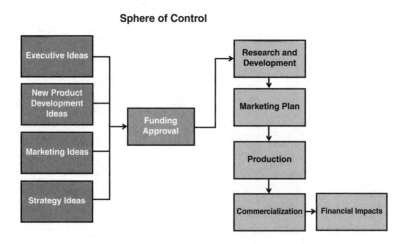

Figure 9.2 Current product development selection process

9.5.3 Upstream and Downstream Interactions

Senior management has grown the business and has been successful in the development of many good products. They select products by gut feeling, which has been good, and the company absorbed financially and operationally any product failures.

Downstream and upstream impacts need to be studied, particularly manufacturing, inventory control, and distribution. The impact of random product development efforts makes it difficult for the efficient use of resources in research personnel, consistent marketing messages, production planning, and logistics. Financial impacts are captured after the fact, rather than creating a financial plan, where some expensive mistakes can be made.

9.5.4 Identification of the Data that Supports the Measurement of the Objectives

After a project is funded, most of the financial requirements associated with the development are determined on an after-the-fact basis. These include the expenditures, the success of the product in the market place, new markets that have been entered, and sales levels for the various products. There is no real feedback loop for the developed products and the resulting financial and operational costs that help determine the degree to which a given product is a "good idea." This means that development of the various products is not systematically captured and used to make better product development selections in the future.

9.6 Data Mining and Statistical Analysis

Key data in this analysis is the financial and market success of the products introduced by the company. Table 9.10 represents the after-the-fact analysis of the products that have been introduced in the last year. Following are the key metrics included in the analysis:

- Market Size - Customer Base
- Number of Customers
- Market Growth Potential
- Average Annual Profit per Customer
- Customer Satisfaction Rating

- After Tax Margin/ROI
- Payback Period (years)
- Net Present Value (millions)
- Technical Development (millions)
- Marketing (millions)
- Operations Investment (millions)

These factors are all good indicators of the success of the product introduction. Some product options have an after tax return on investment as low as 2 percent and others as high as 32 percent. Nearly $100 million has been invested in product development throughout the year. A more structured, consistent approach to product development and an estimated future value can lead to higher overall profitability for the company.

If the products were evaluated prior to the investment into a particular product, you could avoid failures and greatly benefit the company. This then leads to the need for a structured new product development process to incorporate all these considerations consistently in the evaluation process.

9.7 Solve the Problem and Measure the Results

The first step in developing an enhanced process for evaluating new products is to ensure the process includes a standard approach to submit ideas for evaluation to make the best case analysis for each product. This requires a standardized presentation of the information submitted for the selections, evaluating the ideas with input from the key corporate stakeholders, selecting the ideas to pursue, and evaluating the performance of the new products after they have been launched and providing that feedback to the selection process. Figure 9.3 shows a high-level view of the new process.

Table 9.10 Metrics for Data Analysis

Product Evaluation

Products Launched	Market Size – Customer Base	Number of Customers	Market Growth Potential	Average Annual Profit per Customer	Customer Satisfaction Rating	After Tax Margin/ ROI	Payback Period (years)	Net Present Value (millions)	Technical Development (millions)	Marketing (millions)	Operations Investment (millions)
Product A	71,000	65,325	8%	$ 1,595	71.00%	21%	3.6	$ 11.4	$ 1.0	$ 2.8	$ 2.9
Product B	153,000	62,645	59%	$ 1,096	64.00%	11%	3.6	$ 14.0	$ 4.8	$ 2.3	$ 3.8
Product C	93,000	16,384	82%	$ 1,755	95.00%	25%	3.7	$ 20.0	$ 5.7	$ 2.6	$ 2.8
Product A Upgrade	174,000	30,021	83%	$ 997	94.00%	18%	4.2	$ 12.6	$ 3.0	$ 2.1	$ 3.0
Product D	75,000	45,228	40%	$ 1,260	85.00%	8%	2.5	$ 15.1	$ 5.0	$ 2.7	$ 4.9
Product E	110,000	68,844	37%	$ 1,687	71.00%	26%	3.6	$ 12.5	$ 1.0	$ 2.9	$ 1.7
Product B Upgrade	196,000	56,408	71%	$ 1,501	85.00%	6%	2.6	$ 14.0	$ 4.3	$ 4.6	$ 3.3
Product F	138,000	57,252	59%	$ 1,559	68.00%	30%	2.1	$ 18.5	$ 2.2	$ 2.8	$ 2.4
Product G	129,000	79,655	38%	$ 594	82.00%	2%	2.7	$ 9.2	$ 5.0	$ 1.5	$ 2.3
Product H	71,000	65,220	8%	$ 1,387	81.00%	32%	3.0	$ 16.4	$ 2.8	$ 1.5	$ 1.9

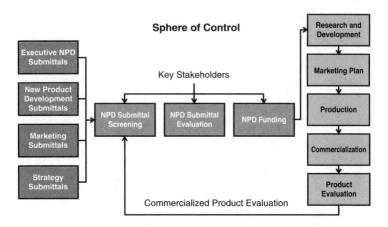

Figure 9.3 Enhanced new product development process

The metrics used to evaluate the new products are based on the objectives and decision criteria established in Section 9.2. These decision criteria represent a comprehensive view of the information needed by the company to launch successful products. The importance of the company objectives and decision criteria is weighted by a consensus of corporate management. With the new process, stakeholders submit ideas via an evaluation form that addresses each of the decision criteria. The submitted projects are evaluated on a quarterly basis to determine which products to pursue. The results of the evaluation are then used to select projects to fund. From here, the research and development activities are used to develop the actual products, which is carried through to decide if commercialization is feasible. After a product has been commercialized, the key metrics shown in the Section 9.5 are evaluated and captured through the screening and evaluation process to include them in the corporate learning experiences. Table 9.11 shows an example of the product evaluations for five different products submitted in the first quarter of the year.

Note when evaluating the criteria for each alternative, it is necessary to use the same scaled data for each criteria. Another approach is to normalize the scale from zero to one for a consistent basis for the evaluation.

Table 9.11 Product Evaluations

Corporate Objectives	Overall Objective Weights	Decision Criteria and Metrics	Decision Criteria Weight	Resulting Criteria Weight	Product 1	Product 2	Product 3	Product 4	Product 5
Enhance Market Position	23%	Ability to Market	5%	1%	2	3	5	5	2
		New/Existing Market	5%	1%	1	2	2	1	2
		Market Attractiveness	10%	2%	3	5	3	4	3
		Market Size of Potential	20%	5%	3	3	5	1	5
		Market Growth Potential	20%	5%	2	1	4	2	5
		Number of Potential Customers	20%	5%	4	4	2	4	2
		Profitability of Customers	10%	2%	1	1	2	1	2
		Customer Satisfaction with Current Products	10%	2%	2	1	3	4	4
Maximize Profit	28%	After Tax Margin/ROI	40%	11%	2	1	4	2	5
		Payback Period	25%	7%	4	5	1	2	1
		Net Present Value	35%	10%	1	1	5	5	3

continues

Table 9.11 Product Evaluations, continued

Corporate Objectives	Overall Objective Weights	Decision Criteria and Metrics	Decision Criteria Weight	Resulting Criteria Weight	Product 1	Product 2	Product 3	Product 4	Product 5
Maximize Resource Utilization	17%	Technical Development Requirements	25%	4%	3	3	4	5	5
		Market Resource Requirements	20%	3%	1	2	3	5	3
		Fits our Production Processes/Equipment	30%	5%	4	5	1	2	3
		Build to Advantage on One or More Strengths	25%	4%	4	2	1	4	2
Maximize the Probability of Success	16%	Probability of Technical Success	50%	8%	3	5	3	2	3
		Probability of Commercial Success	50%	8%	3	2	3	2	5
Strategic Alignment	16%	Strategic Alignment	25%	4%	1	5	4	2	5
		Size of Competitive Barriers	20%	3%	4	5	5	5	5
		Sustainability of Barriers	15%	2%	4	1	1	5	3
		Competitors Attacked	10%	2%	1	2	5	4	2
		Intensity of Competition	10%	2%	4	2	1	2	3
		Opportunity to Obtain Price Premium	10%	2%	1	5	2	2	2
		Product Advantage to Customer Versus Competition	10%	2%	5	2	2	5	3
Product Score					2.64	2.80	3.13	2.99	3.51

The decision criteria After Tax Margin/ROI, Payback Period, Net Present Value, Probability of Technical Success, and Probability of Commercial Success have been computed or assessed and then translated into a 1 to 5 scale which enables you to use the Simple Additive Weight Method for evaluation.

The results show the products by preference ranking. Based on available funds, these product development efforts should be funded in the order shown in Table 9.12. At times, there may be specific products that must be developed due to government mandates, emergency needs, and so on. These products should, however, be evaluated in the same manner for reference and captured for corporate learning.

Table 9.12 Product Development Alternative Ranking

Product	Evaluation Score	Preference Ranking
Product 5	3.51	1
Product 3	3.13	2
Product 4	2.99	3
Product 2	2.80	4
Product 1	2.64	5

This approach provides a defensible framework for evaluation. It includes the corporate goals and supporting metrics at the operational level to evaluate the options. The selection process is standardized, and the actual product selections and associated evaluations are captured for further corporate learning. You can perform additional analysis to refine these results and test the sensitivity of the selection process. This is discussed in the following section.

9.8 Evaluate the Results and Do Sensitivity Analysis

In the new product investment process, there are 50 million dollars to invest in the various products. Each of the projects have an investment cost, and based on the ranking, all but Product 1 is funded in this scenario. Table 9.13 shows the products that will be funded based on their investment requirements and the available budget.

Table 9.13 Product Development Budgeting and Sensitivity Analysis

Product	Evaluation Score	Preference Ranking	Investment Cost	Cumulative Budget (Limit $50 million)
Product 5	3.51	1	$15,000,000	$ 15,000,000
Product 3	3.13	2	$13,000,000	$ 28,000,000
Product 4	2.99	3	$10,000,000	$ 38,000,000
Product 2	2.80	4	$ 8,000,000	$ 46,000,000
Product 1	2.64	5	$12,000,000	$ 58,000,000

You can also see, based on the available budget, that either Product 2 or Product 1, but not both, could be funded and still be within the available budget. You need to do some additional evaluation of Products 1 and 2 to ensure that you make the best decision. Perform a sensitivity analysis to determine what may be required to move Product 1 up the list in the preference ranking and chosen for funding using the decision matrix developed in Section 9.6.

After further analysis of Product 1, you find this product has a greater potential for profitability and the capability to obtain a price premium more than previously anticipated. Additionally, because the company is looking for customers in this given market, Product 1 is also more strategically aligned with the ongoing product development goals of the company. Product 1 would be a better choice than Product 2 in the selection scenario. The resulting funding scenario is shown in Table 9.15.

You can perform additional analyses such as this on the base evaluations to ensure that the company funds the best list of product development efforts. The evaluation and budgeting decisions are documented with this process so that funding decisions can be justified and institutional learning can occur from these decisions. This process ensures that the company has a well-structured, well-thought out budgeting process and use of resources.

Table 9.14 Sensitivity of Product Data

Corporate Objectives	Overall Objective Weights	Decision Criteria and Metrics	Decision Criteria Weight	Resulting Criteria Weight	Product 1	Product 2	Product 3	Product 4	Product 5
Enhance Market Position	23%	Ability to Market	5%	1%	2	3	5	5	2
		New/Existing Market	5%	1%	1	2	2	1	2
		Market Attractiveness	10%	2%	3	5	3	4	3
		Market Size of Potential	20%	5%	3	3	5	1	5
		Market Growth Potential	20%	5%	2	1	4	2	5
		Number of Potential Customers	20%	5%	4	4	2	4	2
		Profitability of Customers	10%	2%	4	1	2	1	2
		Customer Satisfaction with Current Products	10%	2%	2	1	3	4	4
Maximize Profit	28%	After Tax Margin/ROI	40%	11%	2	1	4	2	5
		Payback Period	25%	7%	4	5	1	2	1
		Net Present Value	35%	10%	1	1	5	5	3

continues

Table 9.14 Sensitivity of Product Data, continued

Corporate Objectives	Overall Objective Weights	Decision Criteria and Metrics	Decision Criteria Weight	Resulting Criteria Weight	Product 1	Product 2	Product 3	Product 4	Product 5
Maximize Resource Utilization	17%	Technical Development Requirements	25%	4%	3	3	4	5	5
		Market Resource Requirements	20%	3%	1	2	3	5	3
		Fits our Production Processes/Equipment	30%	5%	4	5	1	2	3
		Build to Advantage on One or More Strengths	25%	4%	4	2	1	4	2
Maximize the Probability of Success	16%	Probability of Technical Success	50%	8%	3	5	3	2	3
		Probability of Commercial Success	50%	8%	3	2	3	2	5
Strategic Alignment	16%	Strategic Alignment	25%	4%	4	5	4	2	5
		Size of Competitive Barriers	20%	3%	4	5	5	5	5
		Sustainability of Barriers	15%	2%	4	1	1	5	3
		Competitors Attacked	10%	2%	1	2	5	4	2
		Intensity of Competition	10%	2%	4	2	1	2	3
		Opportunity to Obtain Price Premium	10%	2%	4	5	2	2	2
		Product Advantage to Customer Versus Competition	10%	2%	5	2	2	5	3
Product Score					2.88	2.80	3.13	2.99	3.51

Table 9.15 Sensitivity Analysis

Product	Evaluation Score	Preference Ranking	Investment Cost	Cumulative Budget (Limit $50 million)
Product 5	3.51	1	$15,000,000	$ 15,000,000
Product 3	3.13	2	$13,000,000	$ 28,000,000
Product 4	2.99	3	$10,000,000	$ 38,000,000
Product 1	2.88	4	$12,000,000	$ 50,000,000
Product 2	2.80	5	$ 8,000,000	$ 58,000,000

9.9 Summary

This case study provides an analysis of key considerations for a company that has previously been successful in launching many new products. This company has emerged from a entrepreneurial-focused company into an established corporate entity. A key issue with the company is better use of limited resources. From these analyses using the methods in this chapter, the company now has developed a structured decision process in which corporate objectives are driven into the selection of new products to develop and launch. This new process provides before-the-fact evaluations so that the goals that the company wants to achieve with its new product launches are achieved. The result is a better use of corporate resources, traceability of its decisions, and a tie of its decisions to the corporate goals and performance metrics important to the company. The company can use this structure and process to formalize and support its ongoing success.

10

Airline Merger

10.1 Introduction

This case study applies the methodology described in the book to a problem involving merging two companies. This process assesses whether this merger is a good fit and a good business decision. Two regional airlines are used in this analysis that have similar characteristics and are public companies with available data.

Mergers present an interesting issue because you must assess the performance of each of the companies, determine how they perform independently, determine how they would potentially perform as a combined single entity, and then determine the net financial value of the merger. The step-by-step analyses presented in this book are useful to provide an operational assessment of the merging companies, determine the interactions between the functions, assess the operational impacts and project the financial benefits from this merger.

The data in this assessment was extracted from the Bureau of Transportation Statistics' website, the annual reports for the companies, and the 10-k report submitted to the Security and Exchange Commission (SEC) by each company. This public data is helpful when assessing the viability of mergers and acquisitions because other internal operating information for the companies may not otherwise be available. Subjective data that may also be required for the analysis can be developed by other industry news releases, trade magazines, and past and current employee input. The goal is to assess the operating activities and issues beyond just the financial benefit to avoid unforeseen consequences after the merger is complete. This methodology helps to guide individuals through that thought process prior to committing to the financial decisions.

This case study is based on two regional airline companies. Preliminary analysis of these companies shows that although they both are regional airlines, they have different strategic focus. One of the companies was a regional low-cost carrier. The other company was a regional hub (central scheduling and routing point) that wants to expand (satellite departures and destinations and low-cost carrier) its operations and to enhance its cost competitiveness. Preliminary consideration for merging these two companies are based on the following characteristics associated with the two airlines.

1. **Uniformity of business, services, and products**—The airline industry provides a fairly standard service, which is to transport individuals (or freight) from one destination to another destination. Although the equipment used, operating philosophy, repair in-house or outsourcing, pricing, advertising, and intended markets can be different, in general, similar equipment and procedures are used in this industry. Regional airlines are a subsection of the airline industry and typically have more narrowly defined operating conditions. In this case, the analysis is limited to transporting individuals and does not address goods and material transportation, such as that provided by Federal Express, UPS, and so on.

2. **Established industry**—The airline industry is an established industry. High capital investment, fixed facilities, and basic needs generated by this society make this industry one that has been in business a long time and will most likely stay that way in the future. The profile of operating philosophies has changed, moving from standard, legacy airlines to low-cost carriers, changing services, service levels, and expectations required by individual companies. The industry however, overall, is established and will continue in the future.

3. **Company with new, interesting, and successful approach to business**—One of the greatest success stories in the airline industry is Southwest Airlines. Southwest created and successfully implemented a new image, and its version of the low-cost

carrier business model is one of the best and most stable airlines in the industry. Its new company business model includes working to meet different needs within the market, specifically regional airlines with lower capacity aircraft. Regional airlines are also anticipated to be a high growth component in the airline industry. These regional airlines have a proven track record that you can use to assess their operating trends and characteristics. The two regional airlines have had a different operating focus, so combining the two creates potentially new markets and an expanded customer base.

4. **Accessibility to data and information**—The airline industry is discussed and tracked in business literature and government information. Because the Federal Aviation Administration (FAA) governs this industry, much of the data for safety and other issues are available to the public in databases, and Excel spreadsheets are on the Department of Transportation (DOT), Bureau of Transportation and Statistics (BTS), and FAA websites. The business and government data provide a good base point for doing this analysis.

5. **Knowledge and experience with industry**—Having a background and insight to information about the airline industry provides the expertise to evaluate the operating and cultural characteristics and can be invaluable in merger and acquisition decisions.

Regional airlines represent a sub segment of the overall airline industry and have experienced significant growth in recent years. Public information about the airline industry is available because of the government regulation of this industry. Using the airline industry provided information, you can evaluate specific company performance information.

10.2 Define the Objectives

Typically, there are a number of reasons to undertake a merger. Many times, companies look to increase growth, take advantage of economies of scale, introduce new products or services, and increase overall profitability. The objectives of this merger are of similar nature. One of the regional airlines has a hub-and-spoke operationsand the other airline is an effective low-cost carrier. These two companies have some overlap in the regions that they service, but merging the two companies would improve both of the companies' geographical footprint in the industry.

From this, the executive teams decided on a number of different objectives for the merger. Both companies must come to a consensus on the objectives to be achieved by merging the two companies. These objectives can be used to develop a roadmap for the specific integration activities that will take place with the two companies. The following list shows these objectives.

- **Increase market base**—One of the primary reasons to merge the two companies is to capitalize on the strengths of the two different companies and expand service areas.

- **Reduce operations and information technology costs**— The intent is to reduce the operating infrastructure of the two companies by leveraging the operations and information technology functions.

- **Improve profitability**—Overall, by achieving economies of scale, the goal is to improve the profitability of the two companies with the merger.

- **Improve customer service**—Maintain and improve key areas of customer service by identifying the best business practices of the companies and adopting/implementing those strategies.

- **Ensure strategic alignment**—With a merger, you need to recognize the different corporate cultures of the two companies and ensure that the integrated company can function seamlessly as one new business entity.

The executive teams believe that if these objectives are accomplished, the merger will be a success. It is critical that all key stakeholders understand the path that is being driven for the merger activity. By doing so, specific courses of action can be developed from these objectives to define the key accomplishments required to make the merger successful.

10.3 Developing Decision Criteria and Metrics

Because the airline industry is monitored by the government, airline-related metrics are readily available to the public. The Department of Transportation (DOT) reports, Bureau of Transportation Statistics (BTS), FAA information, and Office of the Inspector General Data, SEC 10-k data, and airline websites were used to identify a number of decision criteria and performance metrics to support the merger objectives. Of the hundreds of financial and operational airline metrics publically tracked, a subset of these decision criteria/metrics was identified to quantify the objectives. Many of the metrics reviewed were related to each other in terms of revenue, cost, and operational characteristics. It was important to identify key metrics used in the industry to characterize the operations and financial position of the two companies. Due to the readily available data, most of the metrics were objective and could be tracked historically for the airline. Some metrics were subjective and were selected to capture the more subjective aspects of a company merger, such as combining different corporate cultures and employees.

10.3.1 Step 1: Establish Overall Objectives and Goals

The executive teams from the two companies developed the objectives of the merger as stated in Section 10.2. These objectives can be used as a foundation for measuring the success of the merger activity.

- Increase market base
- Reduce operations and information technology costs
- Improve profitability
- Improve customer service
- Ensure strategic alignment

10.3.2 Step 2: Weight the Objectives to Determine Their Importance

These objectives were weighted by the executive group by consensus and the resulting objective weights are shown in Table 10.1.

Table 10.1 Objective Weighting

	Objective Weights					
Merger Objectives	**Executive 1**	**Executive 2**	**Executive 3**	**Executive 4**	**Executive 5**	**Overall Weights**
Increase Market Base	20%	30%	25%	20%	20%	23%
Reduce Operations and Information Technology Costs	25%	20%	15%	20%	10%	18%
Improve Profitability	25%	20%	25%	20%	25%	23%
Improve Customer Service	15%	10%	20%	20%	25%	18%
Ensure Strategic Alignment	15%	20%	15%	20%	20%	18%

This input from the executives shows that increasing the market base and profitability are more important to most than the other objectives. None of the objectives, however, had minimal weighting; therefore, keeping focused on all the identified objectives is important to successfully merge the two companies.

10.3.3 Step 3: Select the Decision Criteria

As discussed earlier in this chapter, a number of different airline financial and operating performance metrics were identified to determine how to measure the performance in supporting the objectives. You can use these decision criteria to benchmark each of the company's performance activities against the industry standards. The decision criteria are shown in Table 10.2.

Table 10.2 Decision Criteria

Objectives	Decision Criteria
Increase Market Base	Number of Destinations
	Average Passenger Trip Length
	Percent Market Share
Reduce Operations and Information Technology Costs	Percent of Single Model Aircraft
	Unit Revenue
	Unit Cost
	Passenger Load Factor
	IT System Investment

continues

Table 10.2 Decision Criteria, continued

Objectives	Decision Criteria
Improve Profitability	Revenue Growth
	Age of Fleet (Years)
	Net Operating Profit
Improve Customer Service	Mishandled Baggage
	Customer Complaints
	On-Time Arrivals
Ensure Strategic Alignment	Percent Total Operating Revenue Salaries and Benefits
	Average Employee Tenure
	Strategic Alignment

10.3.4 Step 4: Weight the Criteria to Determine Their Importance

The executive group then weights the decision criteria to indicate their importance. This weighting helps to place focus on specific performance areas to be managed in the merger activities, as shown in Table 10.3.

Table 10.3 Decision Criteria Weighting

Objectives	Objective Weights	Decision Criteria	Decision Criteria Weights	Resulting Criteria Weight
Increase Market Base	23%	Aircraft in Service	20%	5%
		Number of Destinations	30%	7%
		Average Passenger Trip Length	20%	5%
		Percent Market Share	30%	7%
Reduce Operations and Information Technology Costs	18%	Percent of Single Model Aircraft	10%	2%
		Unit Revenue	25%	5%
		Unit Cost	25%	5%
		Passenger Load Factor	25%	5%
		IT System Investment	15%	3%

continues

Table 10.3 Decision Criteria Weighting, continued

Objectives	Objective Weights	Decision Criteria	Decision Criteria Weights	Resulting Criteria Weight
Improve Profitability	23%	Revenue Growth	40%	9%
		Age of Fleet (Years)	30%	7%
		Net Operating Profit	30%	7%
Improve Customer Service	18%	Mishandled Baggage	35%	6%
		Customer Complaints	35%	6%
		On-Time Arrivals	30%	5%
Ensure Strategic Alignment	18%	Percent Total Operating Revenue Salaries and Benefits	35%	6%
		Average Employee Tenure	35%	6%
		Strategic Alignment	30%	5%

10.3.5 Develop Decision Criteria Metrics

Each of the metrics identified are then defined so that they can be used in the performance assessment of each of the objectives. In this case, most of the decision criteria are industry benchmarks. The company can use and assess other subjective decision criteria based on expert opinion and industry knowledge. Table 10.4 shows whether the decision criteria are supported from industry benchmark/objective data or subjective analysis.

Table 10.4 Decision Criteria Definitions

Objectives	Decision Criteria	Definition	Objective or Subjective
Increase Market Base	Aircraft in Service	Number of aircraft in service at the end of the year.	Objective
	Number of Destinations	Number of destinations serviced by the airline.	Objective
	Average Passenger Trip Length	Average length of trip per passenger.	Objective
	Percent Market Share	Number of passengers for airline divided by total number of passengers for 10 largest airlines.	Objective

continues

Table 10.4 Decision Criteria Definitions, continued

Objectives	Decision Criteria	Definition	Objective or Subjective
Reduce Operations and Information Technology Costs	Percent of Single Model Aircraft	Percent of aircraft that are the same model, which can be used as an indicator of maintenance complexity.	Objective
	Unit Revenue	Measure of operating revenue to available seat miles. Available seat miles equal the total number of seats available for transporting passengers during a reporting period multiplied by the total number of miles flown during that period.	Objective
	Unit Cost	Measure of operating cost to available seat miles. Available Seat Miles equal the total number of seats available for transporting passengers during a reporting period multiplied by the total number of miles flown during that period.	Objective
	Passenger Load Factor	Measure of how much of an airline's passenger carrying capacity is used. It is passenger-miles flown as a percentage of seat-miles available.	Objective
	IT System Investment	Yearly dollar investment in information technology infrastructure, which can be used as an indicator of the importance of information technology investment to the company.	Objective
Improve Profitability	Revenue Growth	Percent growth in revenue on a year to year basis.	Objective
	Age of Fleet (Years)	An aircraft's age is based on the number of years since the aircraft's production.	Objective
	Net Operating Profit	Net operating profit represents the profitability of a company after accounting for cost of goods sold and operating expenses, which can be used to represent how well management is doing to grow the profitability of the company.	Objective

continues

Table 10.4 Decision Criteria Definitions, continued

Objectives	Decision Criteria	Definition	Objective or Subjective
Improve Customer Service	Mishandled Baggage	Number of lost bags per thousand passengers.	Objective
	Customer Complaints	Number of complaints per hundred thousand passengers.	Objective
	On-Time Arrivals	Percent of flights arriving within 15 minutes of scheduled arrival time.	Objective
Ensure Strategic Alignment	Percent Total Operating Revenue Salaries and Benefits	Overhead percent of revenue of salaries and benefits.	Objective
	Average Employee Tenure	Average years of service for all employees of the company, which can be used to indicate seniority and adaptability to change.	Objective
	Strategic Alignment	Subjective measure of how well the merging companies have been aligned with operational and management philosophies.	Subjective

Most of the decision criteria specified are readily available in public data tracked and maintained by airlines from a number of government sources. These metrics are relatively easy to capture and maintained on a yearly basis.

10.4 Explore the Environment

After the decision criteria and metrics have been established, you need to analyze the interactions and interdependencies between the various organizational areas in each company and assess the overall organizational impacts with both of the companies combined.

10.4.1 Integrated Corporate Planning

In this case, you perform the Integrated Corporate Planning for each company individually. This can help to point out areas of strength and weaknesses in the individual companies. Next, you model the performance for each of the two different companies combined. This can help to guide merger activities and focus areas to ensure success in merging the two companies.

10.4.1.1 Assess the Scope of the Problem

Basically, all functional areas of both companies will be impacted by the merger activities. Some areas will have a greater impact than other areas and should have more initial focus in the integration efforts. It is key that operations, customer service, profitability, strategic alignment, and marketing are well integrated and that the operational and financial performance is maintained. Therefore, you need to focus on each of the following areas in the primary assessment of the two different companies and the resulting merged company.

- Marketing/Sales
- Operations/Information Technology
- Finance
- Customer Service
- Corporate Strategy

10.4.1.2 Develop the Activity Relationship Matrix

Incorporating the preceding five corporate areas, the activity relationship matrix has been set up and is shown in Table 10.5. The goal of the activity relationship matrix is to capture the interactions between the key functional areas in the company. In this case study, you assess two different regional airlines. From the assessment of the two individual airlines, you can see that the interactions between the functional areas are the same. This is reasonable because there are certain specific operating characteristics that exist within an airline. Because they are similar types of regional airlines, this appears to be true from a high-level functional view of the company. Table 10.5 shows the Activity Relationship Matrix for the regional airline analysis for the two airlines.

Table 10.5 Activity Relationship Matrix

Activity Relationship Matrix–Company 1

From					
Department Listing	**1**	**2**	**3**	**4**	**5**
1. Marketing/Sales		B	A	B	A
				3	
2. Operations/Information Technology			A	A	B
3. Finance				B	A
4. Customer Service					A
5. Corporate Strategy					

Closeness Rating

Value	Closeness	Line Code
A	Absolutely Necessary	═══════
B	Very Important	▬▬▬▬▬
C	Important	────────
D	Unimportant	
E	Undesirable	XXXX

Reason for the Closeness Value

Code	Reason
1	Interrelated Processes
2	Shared Resources
3	Same Management Chain

10.4.1.3 Quantify Performance with Industry Benchmarks and Performance Evaluations

Decision criteria for the two regional airlines are established. These decision criteria relate to the functional areas of the companies.

You can use this consistent set of metrics to assess both airlines and additionally provide a view of the performance level of the individual airlines. The key decision criteria can benchmark the company against other companies in the industry for the various functional areas. Additionally, these individual company performance metrics can assess which functional areas of the companies might be adapted as the best business practices and processes with the merged company and areas of improvement across both companies. This activity provides insight into key areas of focus with the merger activities. Table 10.6 shows the decision criteria/industry benchmark assessment for both companies.

Table 10.6 Benchmark Performance for Company 1

Performance Assessment from Corporate Priorities–Company 1

	Decision Criteria	Benchmark Performance (1 high–5 low)	Aggregated Benchmark Performance (1 high–5 low)
1. Marketing/ Sales	Aircraft in Service	3	3.25
	Number of Destinations	3	
	Average Passenger Trip Length	4	
	Percent Market Share	3	
2. Operations/ Information Technology	Percent of Single Model Aircraft	2	2.60
	Unit Revenue	3	
	Unit Cost	2	
	Passenger Load Factor	3	
	IT System Investment	3	
3. Finance	Revenue Growth	4	3.00
	Age of Fleet (Years)	3	
	Net Operating Profit	2	
4. Customer Service	Mishandled Baggage	2	2.00
	Customer Complaints	2	
	On-Time Arrivals	2	

continues

Table 10.6 Benchmark Performance for Company 1, continued

Performance Assessment from Corporate Priorities–Company 1

	Decision Criteria	Benchmark Performance (1 high–5 low)	Aggregated Benchmark Performance (1 high–5 low)
5. Corporate Strategy	Percent Total Operating Revenue Salaries and Benefits	3	3.00
	Average Employee Tenure	3	
	Strategic Alignment	3	

The performance assessments differ for Company 2, as shown in Table 10.7.

Table 10.7 Benchmark Performance for Company 2

Performance Assessment from Corporate Priorities–Company 2

	Decision Criteria	Benchmark Performance (1 high–5 low)	Aggregated Benchmark Performance (1 high–5 low)
1. Marketing/ Sales	Aircraft in Service	3	3.25
	Number of Destinations	3	
	Average Passenger Trip Length	4	
	Percent Market Share	3	
2. Operations/ Information Technology	Percent of Single Model Aircraft	2	2.60
	Unit Revenue	3	
	Unit Cost	2	
	Passenger Load Factor	4	
	IT System Investment	2	
3. Finance	Revenue Growth	5	3.67
	Age of Fleet (Years)	3	
	Net Operating Profit	3	
4. Customer Service	Mishandled Baggage	3	2.67
	Customer Complaints	2	
	On-Time Arrivals	3	

continues

Table 10.7 Benchmark Performance for Company 2, continued

Performance Assessment from Corporate Priorities–Company 2			
	Decision Criteria	Benchmark Performance (1 high–5 low)	Aggregated Benchmark Performance (1 high–5 low)
5. Corporate Strategy	Percent Total Operating Revenue Salaries and Benefits	4	3.33
	Average Employee Tenure	3	
	Strategic Alignment	3	

10.4.1.4 Develop the Activity Relationship Diagram

The Activity Relationship Diagram is developed to account for the functional interactions along with the magnitude of the issues assessed against the industry benchmarks. In this case, we have grouped the functional areas for the two companies and have represented their benchmark performance and interactions in the Activity Relationship Diagram, as shown in Figure 10.1. This was done so that we could evaluate the interactions between the functions in the two companies and also then evaluate focus areas and courses of action that can be taken with the merger and the project planning to accomplish the merger.

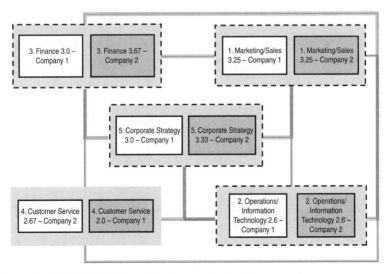

Figure 10.1 Activity Relationship diagram for both companies

The diagram is constructed so that the areas with the greatest need for improvement and the closeness of the functions are shown at the top of the diagram. This creates a visual representation of the areas so that management can focus on productivity improvement efforts. It is important as well to represent the closeness of the relationships so that the interactions between functions are captured in process enhancements. Corporate knowledge can then be used to identify specific improvement opportunities.

From the activity relationship diagram, the areas of focus for the merger become evident. It appears that the Customer Service and Operations/Information Technology functions in both of the companies are performing slightly above the Department of Transportation's industry averages and benchmark values. Further evaluation would be required to determine if these functions for both of the companies could be easily integrated. It also shows that the possibility exists that one or the other company's procedures may be selected as an adopt-and-go strategy, phasing out the functions of one company and utilizing the other company's capabilities. Both Customer Service and Operations/IT are, however, linked strongly to the overall corporate and merger strategy, so that needs to be accounted for in ongoing merger decisions.

The areas of Finance and Marketing/Sales for both of the companies are at or below industry standards. Preliminarily, this shows that focus should be placed in both of these areas in the merger activities. Additionally, the Corporate Strategy appears to be key to operational functions. The activities to support the corporate strategies are an important part of a successful merger.

10.4.1.5 Identify Specific Problem Areas to Improve

You can also assess additional data to provide insights into areas of focus for the merger. In this case, historical data was gathered for each of the airlines over a multiple year time horizon. These data are then analyzed to determine the company averages, variability, and current industry standard performance levels for each of the decision criteria. Additionally, a statistical measure called the coefficient of variation, which is a normalized indicator of the extent of variability in a metric, was used to assess the degree of variability associated with the individual metrics. Since the performance measures have different units of measure, the coefficient of variation provides a unit neutral way, a percentage, to view variability impacts. This measure identifies performance inconsistencies that can be improved with the reduction in the variability. These statistics were aggregated to determine the variability associated with the performance indicators for the functional areas. Table 10.8 shows an example of this information.

The data collected from Company 1 and Company 2 is shown in Tables 10.9 and 10.10. You can use this high-level set of performance metrics to develop benchmark measures and variability measures, and to assess the percent of the total budget that each area impacts.

In many situations, just gathering this information is quite helpful for decision making. The detailed performance information provides decision makers with the ability to pinpoint specific areas of high and low performance. This information can then be aggregated to a high-level view of performance for each of the functional areas. The results of the variability analysis and percent budget analysis for the two companies are shown in Tables 10.11 and 10.12.

Both companies have higher variability and higher coefficient of variation within their Finance functions. Special attention is needed in merging the two companies in the area of Finance to ensure success. Additionally, Corporate Strategy has higher variability and coefficient of variation in the area of Corporate Strategy for Company 1, and Marketing/Sales has higher variability in Company 2.

Table 10.8 Variability Analysis Example

	Decision Criteria	2002	2003	2004	2005
2. Operations/ Information Technology	Percent of Single Model Aircraft	70.1%	72.2%	70.1%	65.8%
	Unit Revenue	7.71	7.32	6.69	7.18
	Unit Cost	6.43	6.08	6.04	6.91
	Passenger Load Factor	83.00%	84.50%	83.20%	85.20%
	IT System Investment	$ 25.8	$ 60.7	$ 44.9	$ 48.2

Table 10.9 Company 1 Data

	Decision Criteria	2002	2003	2004	2005
1. Marketing/ Sales	Aircraft in Service	65	74	87	105
	Number of Destinations	39	43	53	51
	Average Passenger Trip Length	245	252	313	320
	Percent Market Share	5.0%	5.2%	5.9%	6.5%
2. Operations/ Information Technology	Percent of Single Model Aircraft	56.0%	57.9%	59.0%	55.4%
	Unit Revenue	8.88	9.14	8.47	9.43
	Unit Cost	8.51	8.28	8.45	9.28
	Passenger Load Factor	67.60%	71.10%	70.80%	73.50%
	IT System Investment	$10.40	$33.80	$33.40	$37.00
3. Finance	Revenue Growth	13%	25.2%	10.5%	42.9%
	Age of Fleet (Years)	9	3	3	3
	Net Operating Profit	$10.70	$100.50	$10.10	$8.10
4. Customer Service	Mishandled Baggage	2.70	1.95	3.70	2.93
	Customer Complaints	0.55	0.40	0.69	0.61
	On-time Arrivals	80.2%	81.4%	82.7%	82.6%
5. Corporate Strategy	Percent Total Operating Revenue Salaries and Benefits	27.7%	25.2%	27.0%	22.7%
	Average Employee Tenure	7.6	6.6	6.0	4.3
	Strategic Alignment				

2006	2007	2008	2009	Mean	Std Dev	CV	Industry Average
70.6%	69.5%	71.2%	70.7%	70.0%	1.9%	2.7%	50%
8.26	8.91	10.44	10.09	8.3	1.4	16.6%	10.11
7.76	8.27	9.87	8.99	7.5	1.4	18.8%	9.50
81.60%	80.70%	80.40%	79.70%	82.3%	0.0	2.4%	81%
$ 69.9	$ 83.4	$ 56.1	$113.6	$62.8	26.7	42.6%	$ 57.7

2006	2007	2008	2009	Mean	Std Dev	CV
127	137	136	138	108.6	30.1	27.7%
53	64	84	85	59.0	17.4	29.5%
336	384	396	395	330.1	60.0	18.2%
5.1%	6.3%	6.9%	5.1%	5.8%	0.7%	13.0%
56.2%	58.4%	55.5%	62.9%	57.7%	2.5%	4.4%
9.95	10.18	10.72	10.05	9.6	0.8	7.8%
9.74	9.55	11.04	9.29	9.3	0.9	9.7%
72.80%	76.20%	79.60%	79.80%	73.9%	4.3%	5.9%
$31.20	$31.80	$33.50	$54.40	33.2	11.9	35.8%
30.5%	22.1%	10.5%	-8.3%	18.3%	15.5%	84.5%
3	4	5	6	4.5	2.1	47.5%
$15.50	$50.50	($266.30)	$134.70	$7.98	120.5	1511.6%
3.75	3.80	2.62	3.48	3.1	0.7	21.5%
0.57	0.64	0.41	0.53	0.5	0.1	18.7%
81.6%	82.5%	81.0%	80.2%	82%	1.0%	1.3%
20.6%	19.6%	18.6%	20.9%	22.8%	3.5%	15.2%
7.7	3.9	4.0	5.0	5.6	1.6	27.7%

Table 10.10 Company 2 Data

	Decision Criteria	2002	2003	2004	2005
1. Marketing/ Sales	Aircraft in Service	37	53	69	92
	Number of Destinations	48	48	64	64
	Average Passenger Trip Length	264	270	249	213
	Percent Market Share	6.3%	6.1%	5.7%	5.7%
2. Operations/ Information Technology	Percent of Single Model Aircraft	70.1%	72.2%	70.1%	65.8%
	Unit Revenue	7.71	7.32	6.69	7.18
	Unit Cost	6.43	6.08	6.04	6.91
	Passenger Load Factor	83.00%	84.50%	83.20%	85.20%
	IT System Investment	$ 25.8	$ 60.7	$ 44.9	$ 48.2
3. Finance	Revenue Growth	30%	57.2%	26.7%	34.5%
	Age of Fleet (Years)	5	3.67	4.9	5.4
	Net Operating Profit	$55.00	$103.00	$46.00	($25.00)
4. Customer Service	Mishandled Baggage	3.40	3.55	2.65	3.63
	Customer Complaints	0.53	0.78	0.46	0.80
	On-time Arrivals	81.0%	79.7%	79.0%	80.9%
5. Corporate Strategy	Percent Total Operating Revenue Salaries and Benefits	25.50%	26.80%	26.60%	25.10%
	Average Employee Tenure	4.2	4.9	4.7	4.4
	Strategic Alignment				

2006	2007	2008	2009	Mean	Std Dev	CV
119	134	142	151	99.6	43.2	43.4%
63	66	81	106	67.5	18.8	27.8%
228	278	356	393	281.4	62.2	22.1%
6.2%	6.3%	6.2%	5.3%	6.0%	0.4%	6.1%
70.6%	69.5%	71.2%	70.7%	70.0%	1.9%	2.7%
8.26	8.91	10.44	10.09	8.3	1.4	16.6%
7.76	8.27	9.87	8.99	7.5	1.4	18.8%
81.60%	80.70%	80.40%	79.70%	82.3%	0.0	2.4%
$ 69.9	$ 83.4	$ 56.1	$113.6	$ 62.8	26.7	42.6%
38.9%	20.3%	19.2%	-3.0%	28.0%	17.4%	62.2%
5.6	6	4.8	4.7	5.0	0.7	14.0%
($7.00)	$12.00	($85.00)	$58.00	$19.63	58.6	298.8%
2.67	3.71	3.76	3.80	3.4	0.5	13.9%
0.60	0.41	0.48	0.76	0.6	0.2	26.3%
80.1%	78.9%	78.4%	78.3%	80%	1.1%	1.3%
23.40%	22.80%	20.50%	23.60%	24.3%	2.1%	8.7%
4.5	5.8	5.0	4.2	4.7	0.5	11.2%

Table 10.11 Activity Relationship Matrix for Company 1

From					
Department Listing	**1**	**2**	**3**	**4**	**5**
1. Marketing/Sales		B	A	B	A
				3	
2. Operations/Information Technology			A	A	B
3. Finance				B	A
4. Customer Service					A
5. Corporate Strategy					

Table 10.12 Activity Relationship Matrix for Company 2

From					
Department Listing	**1**	**2**	**3**	**4**	**5**
1. Marketing/Sales		B	A	B	A
2. Operations/Information Technology			A	A	B
3. Finance				B	A
4. Customer Service					A
5. Corporate Strategy					

Aggregated Benchmark Performance (1 high - 5 low)	Variability - Fuzzy or Statistical	Percent of Total Budget
3.25	Medium	20%
2.60	Low	40%
3.00	High	10%
2.00	Medium	25%
3.00	High	5%

Aggregated Benchmark Performance (1 high - 5 low)	Variability - Fuzzy or Statistical	Percent of Total Budget
3.25	High	20%
2.60	Medium	45%
3.67	High	10%
2.67	Medium	20%
3.33	Medium	5%

From this analysis, areas of primary importance need to focus on stabilizing the Marketing/Sales, Finance, and Corporate Strategy functions without sacrificing the existing performance levels in Operations/IT and Customer Service. Significant, specific efforts in key functional areas will be required for a successful merger. Figure 10.2 shows the Activity Relationship diagram with the key focus areas.

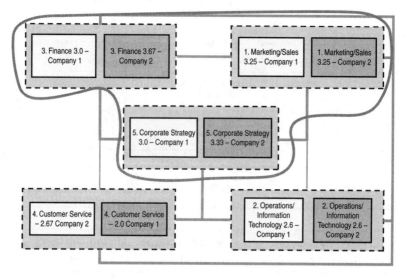

Figure 10.2 Merger focus areas

10.5 Explore the Scope of the Problem and Its Importance

Careful analyses are necessary to identify problem areas.

10.5.1 Identification of the Problem Areas

The problem areas in this merger are two-fold. First, you need to integrate the functions from the different operational areas to provide one seamless operational company. Second, the merged company must enhance those performance areas operating below the industry standards. Both activities are important. Change associated with a merger provides an opportunity to combine functions in such a way to enhance the processes. These key opportunity areas must be explored and an action plan developed to result in a "better than before" operating company.

To begin this analysis, an inventory of the functional areas for the two companies should be taken to assess the key activities that need to be addressed in the merger. Table 10.13 shows a high-level view of this analysis. The decision criteria for each objective are first related to specific operational areas that can be analyzed for integration activities and performance improvements. These operational areas affect the decision criteria performance. Additionally, these operational areas can be used to evaluate the commonalties and differences between the companies, develop the integration strategy for the merger, and project the future financial outcomes of the merged companies. The operating functions shown in this table differ from the decision criteria that have been established. You can link these functional activities to the decision criteria/metrics that can drive the successful performance of each of these areas.

10.5.2 Definition of the Sphere of Control

In the merger, the sphere of control encompasses all the critical areas of the company. Activities involve the development of various corporate strategies related to specific areas of the company, the adoption of best business practices from one of the companies in certain areas, and operational assessment and process improvement in other areas of the company. Figure 10.3 shows a high-level representation of the types of operational activities that should take place and the overall interactions and impact across the various areas of the company. Specific analyses in each of the areas are required to develop the merger activities and action plans.

Table 10.13 Operational Area Assessments

	Decision Criteria	**Operational Areas**
1. Marketing/Sales	Aircraft in Service	Customer Volume
	Number of Destinations	Geographic Coverage
	Average Passenger Trip Length	Hub and Spoke
	Percent Market Share	Target Market
2. Operations/ Information Technology	Percent of Single Model Aircraft	Maintenance and Training
	Unit Revenue	Pricing Models
	Unit Cost	Operational Processes
	Passenger Load Factor	Scheduling and Optimization
	IT System Investment	Purchasing, Ticketing and Scheduling
3. Finance	Revenue Growth	Investment in Long Term Strategy
	Age of Fleet (Years)	Aircraft Replacement Strategy
	Net Operating Profit	Operational Cost Reduction and Price Premiums
4. Customer Service	Mishandled Baggage	Baggage and Cargo Systems
	Customer Complaints	Customer Service Practices
	On-time Arrivals	Gate and Hub Processes
5. Corporate Strategy	Percent Total Operating Revenue Salaries and Benefits	Salary and Benefits Practices
	Average Employee Tenure	Employee Flexibility and Retention
	Strategic Alignment	Similarity in Operating Philosophies

Similarity and Differences Between Company 1 and Company 2	Merged Company
Common - 25%	75% Combined Volume
Common - 10%	90% Combined Geographic Area
Different	Develop New Hub and Spoke Service Map
Common - 25%	Develop New Combined Marketing Message
Common - 50%	Combine Company 1 and 2 Core Competencies
Different	Develop New Combined Pricing Strategy
Common - 75%	Adopt Best Practices
Similar	Adopt Best Practices
Similar	Adopt Best Practices
Different	Develop New Long Term Growth Strategy
Similar	Adopt Best Practices
Common - 50%	Develop New Finance Strategy
Similar	Adopt Best Practices
Similar	Adopt Best Practices
Similar	Adopt Best Practices
Common - 75%	Develop Consistent Salary and Benefit Practices
Similar	Adopt Best Practices
Similar	Develop Consistent Operating Philosophies

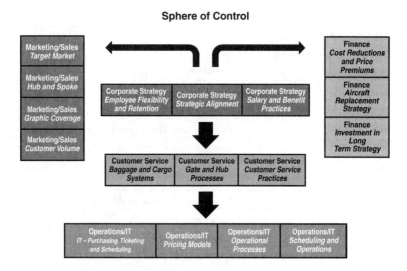

Figure 10.3 Airline merger corporate impacts

10.5.3 Upstream and Downstream Interactions

The overall impacts of various actions to all areas of the company must be accounted for in the activities. All critical areas should be incorporated in the strategic decisions made for the merger. Impacts and interactions with the five functional areas identified earlier in this case study are key to a successful merger. Sales/Marketing, Corporate Strategy, and Finance have been identified as opportunity areas for improvement. Changes to these organizations, however, should not negatively impact the higher performance areas of Operations/IT and Customer Service. The action plans developed should support the overall objective of a successful merger.

10.5.4 Identification of the Data that Supports the Measurement of the Objectives

Data that supports the measurement of the objectives comes in three separate forms. The decision criteria that support the merger objectives have been translated into performance metrics for each of the five key functional areas of the company. Historical data from the years of 2002 through 2009 was gathered for the performance metrics that support the decision criteria and objectives. You can use this data to evaluate historical performance trends and project potential future operational performance for the two merged companies.

Additionally, Section 10.4.1 uses the performance metrics by functional area to identify operational areas that need adoption of best practices, process improvements, or the development of new strategies. For each of these operational areas, costs and benefits will be incurred when developing and implementing the activities in the integration effort. These activities can positively and negatively impact the bottom line financial value of the company.

This leads to a third set of information that you need to evaluate to determine the impact of the integration effort, which is the net resulting Discounted Cash Flow Valuation of the company through and after the integration effort. Hard dollars and projections can be made such that the costs and benefits can be projected for a 5-year time frame that you can then use to evaluate the corporate value after the merger. You can also use this activity to translate those changes to operational metrics into dollar value benefits.

10.6 Data Mining and Statistical Analysis

The performance, integration, and operational data for the two airlines were evaluated. Requirements and activities are identified to determine the net impacts required for the successful merger. Each of the operational areas that link to the key decision criteria are analyzed, and an estimate is made for the additional revenues, expenses, and investment that are necessary for the merger. This analysis will drive the costs, benefits, and projected financial outcomes of the combined companies. This provides a financial assessment of the impacts that are used to determine the resulting Discounted Cash Flow associated with the company merger, as shown in Table 10.14.

Table 10.14 Financial Impacts of Merger (in millions)

| | | | Operational Areas | | |
| | | | Customer Volume | Geographic Coverage | Hub and Spoke |
Year	Category	NOP/ Investment	75% Combined Volume	90% Combined Geographic Area	Develop New Hub and Spoke Service Map
2011	Revenue	$ 285.78	$ 269.78		
	Expense	$ 174.62	$ 115.62		$ 3.00
	Investment	$ 48.00			
	Net Op Profit	$ 111.16			
2012	Revenue	$ 291.36	$ 291.36		
	Expense	$ 131.40	$ 121.40		
	Investment	$ 63.00			
	Net Op Profit	$ 159.96			
2013	Revenue	$ 320.50	$ 320.50		
	Expense	$ 127.47	$ 127.47		
	Investment	$ 45.00			
	Net Op Profit	$ 193.03			
2014	Revenue	$ 352.55	$ 352.55		
	Expense	$ 133.84	$ 133.84		
	Investment	$ 30.00			
	Net Op Profit	$ 218.70			
2015	Revenue	$ 387.80	$ 387.80		
	Expense	$ 140.54	$ 140.54		
	Investment	$ 30.00			
	Net Op Profit	$ 247.27			

Target Market	Maintenance and Training	Pricing Models	Operational Processes	Scheduling and Optimization	Purchasing, Ticketing, and Scheduling
Develop New Combined Marketing Message	Combine Company 1 and 2 Core Competencies	Develop New Combined Pricing Strategy	Adopt Best Practices	Adopt Best Practices	Adopt Best Practices
$ 4.00		$ 10.00		$ 2.00	
$ 10.00	$ 4.00	$ 4.00	$ 1.00	$ 3.00	$ 4.00
				$ 3.00	$ 5.00
	$ 2.00			$ 2.00	
				$ 3.00	$ 5.00

continues

Table 10.14 Financial Impacts of Merger (in millions), continued

Year	Category	NOP/ Investment	Investment in Long Term Strategy — Develop New Long Term Growth Strategy	Aircraft Replacement Strategy — Adopt Best Practices	Operational Cost Reduction and Price Premiums — Develop New Finance Strategy
2011	Revenue	$ 285.78			
	Expense	$ 174.62	$ 2.00		$ 5.00
	Investment	$ 48.00		$ 30.00	
	Net Op Profit	$ 111.16			
2012	Revenue	$ 291.36			
	Expense	$ 131.40			$ 3.00
	Investment	$ 63.00		$ 50.00	
	Net Op Profit	$ 159.96			
2013	Revenue	$ 320.50			
	Expense	$ 127.47			
	Investment	$ 45.00		$ 45.00	
	Net Op Profit	$ 193.03			
2014	Revenue	$ 352.55			
	Expense	$ 133.84			
	Investment	$ 30.00		$ 30.00	
	Net Op Profit	$ 218.70			
2015	Revenue	$ 387.80			
	Expense	$ 140.54			
	Investment	$ 30.00		$ 30.00	
	Net Op Profit	$ 247.27			

Baggage and Cargo Systems	Customer Service Practices	Gate and Hub Processes	Salary and Benefits Practices	Employee Flexibility and Retention	Similarity in Operating Philosophies
Adopt Best Practices	Adopt Best Practices	Adopt Best Practices	Develop Consistent Salary and Benefit Practices	Adopt Best Practices	Develop Consistent Operating Philosophies
$ 10.00	$ 5.00	$ 3.00	$ 10.00	$ 1.00	$ 4.00
$ 5.00	$ 2.00	$ 1.00			

Based on the information in Table 10.3, the financial factors are adjusted to reflect the merged company impacts. It is anticipated that there will be costs the first year associated with assessing and developing the actions required to develop new strategies, integrating maintenance activities to reduce operational costs with best practices, and equalizing the employee base for salaries and benefits. Revenue will be generated from combining the two company customer volume, implementing a new marketing message and pricing strategy, and optimizing the scheduling. Additional investment will be required in computer systems and equipment. The second year, there will be some residual costs and investments associated with the merger. All other revenue and expenses will be captured within the overall operating expenses. Beyond that, it is anticipated that due to the new fleet replacement strategy, there will be additional fleet investments for the post merger 5-year period. You an use this assessment to generate a Discounted Cash Flow for the merged company.

10.7 Solve the Problem and Measure the Results

Integrating all the analyses together, you can generate a high-level Discounted Cash Flow (DCF) to measure the value of the company from the merger activities, as shown in Table 10.15. Analysts use DCF to determine a company's current value according to its estimated future cash flows. Based on the revenue, expense, and investment analysis in the previous section, a discounted cash flow has been calculated for the merged company. A definition of the terms used in the analysis follows the Discounted Cash Flow in Table 10.15.

Table 10.15 Discounted Cash Flow Terminology (dollars in millions)

Prediction Year for Company A	New Company 2011	New Company 2012	New Company 2013	New Company 2014	New Company 2015
1	Net Operating Profit by Year	$111.2	$160.0	$193.0	$218.7	$247.3
2	Estimated Amortization	$15	$15	$17	$19	$22
3	Operating Earnings Before Interest, Taxes and Amortization (EBITA)	$126	$175	$210	$238	$269
4	Taxes on EBITA (35%)	$44	$61	$74	$83	$94
5	Changes in Deferred Taxes	($25)	($23)	($19)	($22)	($22)
6	Net Operating Profit Less Accumulated Taxes (NOPLAT)	$57	$91	$118	$133	$153
7	Net Investment	($48)	($63)	($45)	($30)	($30)
8	Free Cash Flow	$9	$28	$73	$103	$123
9	Weighted Average Cost of Capital (WACC)	5.00%	5.00%	5.00%	5.00%	5.00%
10	Present Value of Cash Flows	$9	$26	$66	$89	$101
11	Total Present Value of Cash Flows in 5-Year Planning Horizon	$291				

continues

Table 10.15 Discounted Cash Flow Terminology (dollars in millions), continued

1. Net Operating Profit (millions)—Normal Operating Revenues minus Normal Operating Expenses

2. Estimated Amortization—Amortization is included in the NOP projection, so it must be removed from the prediction.

3. Operating Earnings Before Interest, Taxes and Amortization (EBITA)—This is the operating earning before interest, taxes, and amortization with amortization removed from the prediction from the fuzzy logic control model.

4. Taxes on EBITA (39%)—Taxes on EBITA were determined by using an estimated tax rate of 39% applied to EBITA.

5. Changes in Deferred Taxes—Changes to the deferred taxes referred to actual income taxes adjusted to a cash basis.

6. Net Operating Profit Less Accumulated Taxes (NOPLAT)—This represents the after-tax operating profits of the company after adjusting the taxes to a cash basis.

7. Net Investment—Net investment is the change in invested capital. Invested capital is the capital invested in the company by shareholders and creditors and operating and other non-operating activities.

8. Free Cash Flow (FCF)—Free cash flow is a company's true operating cash flow. It is the total after-tax cash flow generated by the company to all providers of the company's capital.

9. Weighted Average Cost of Capital (WACC)—The opportunity costs to all the capital providers weighted by their relative contribution to the company's total capital.

10. Present Value of Cash Flows—This is the free cash flows discounted to the present value using the WACC as the discount rate.

11. Total Present Value of Cash Flows in 5-Year Planning Horizon—Sum of cash flows for 5-year planning horizon.

The Discounted Cash Flow analysis shows a positive Net Present Value for the merger over the 5-year planning horizon. The Free Cash Flow steadily increases over the planning horizon as well. Based on the analysis, it appears that the merger of the two companies will be a profitable activity. Certain assumptions, however, have been made for the revenue, expenses, and investment for each of the different operational areas identified in the previous section. These assumptions should be tested to determine their sensitivity and the potential impacts to the resulting company valuation.

10.8 Evaluate the Results and Do Sensitivity Analysis

You need to test the sensitivity of the assumptions made in the DCF. Assume that you predicted the additional operating revenue and operating expenses correctly and assume that any additional revenue (savings) you expected by combining the two companies was realized. However, also assume that the investment remained constant, but the expenses that you anticipated doubled. Table 10.16 shows the operational area financial impacts table previously developed but with the increased expenses. Table 10.17 shows a variety of economic metrics to measure the possibility of success.

You can see that the merged company still has a positive Discounted Cash Flow; however, the company is anticipated to operate at a loss the first year. This could easily be anticipated with a merger.

Now also assume that you were incorrect in your fleet investment requirements, and that they increased by 50% of the estimated investment cost for each of the years. The results would still be a positive business value; however, it would not be until the third year until the company would see a positive Free Cash Flow. Table 10.18 shows the results.

The sensitivity analysis provides a means to understand the impacts of the assumptions made in the analyses and the potential financial consequences if these assumptions do not hold true. This type of analysis can provide confidence in the decisions being made for the merger.

Table 10.16 Sensitivity Analysis with Increased Expenses (in millions)

			Operational Areas		
			Customer Volume	Geographic Coverage	Hub and Spoke
Year	Category	NOP/ Investment	75% Combined Volume	90% Combined Geographic Area	Develop New Hub and Spoke Service Map
2011	Revenue	$ 285.78	$ 269.78		
	Expense	$ 237.62	$ 115.62		$ 6.00
	Investment	$ 48.00			
	Net Op Profit	$ 48.16			
2012	Revenue	$ 291.36	$ 291.36		
	Expense	$ 138.40	$ 121.40		
	Investment	$ 63.00			
	Net Op Profit	$ 152.96			
2013	Revenue	$ 320.50	$ 320.50		
	Expense	$ 127.47	$ 127.47		
	Investment	$ 45.00			
	Net Op Profit	$ 193.03			
2014	Revenue	$ 352.55	$ 352.55		
	Expense	$ 133.84	$ 133.84		
	Investment	$ 30.00			
	Net Op Profit	$ 218.70			
2015	Revenue	$ 387.80	$ 387.80		
	Expense	$ 140.54	$ 140.54		
	Investment	$ 30.00			
	Net Op Profit	$ 247.27			

Target Market	Maintenance and Training	Pricing Models	Operational Processes	Scheduling and Optimization	Purchasing, Ticketing, and Scheduling
Develop New Combined Marketing Message	Combine Company 1 and 2 Core Competencies	Develop New Combined Pricing Strategy	Adopt Best Practices	Adopt Best Practices	Adopt Best Practices
$ 4.00		$ 10.00		$ 2.00	
$ 20.00	$ 8.00	$ 8.00	$ 2.00	$ 6.00	$ 8.00
				$ 3.00	$ 5.00
	$ 4.00			$ 4.00	
				$ 3.00	$ 5.00

continues

Table 10.16 Sensitivity Analysis with Increased Expenses, in millions, continued

| Year | Category | NOP/ Investment | Investment in Long Term Strategy | Aircraft Replacement Strategy | Operational Cost Reduction and Price Premiums |
			Develop New Long Term Growth Strategy	Adopt Best Practices	Develop New Finance Strategy
2011	Revenue	$ 285.78			
	Expense	$ 237.62	$ 8.00		$ 10.00
	Investment	$ 48.00		$ 30.00	
	Net Op Profit	$ 48.16			
2012	Revenue	$ 291.36			
	Expense	$ 138.40			$ 3.00
	Investment	$ 63.00		$ 50.00	
	Net Op Profit	$ 152.96			
2013	Revenue	$ 320.50			
	Expense	$ 127.47			
	Investment	$ 45.00		$ 45.00	
	Net Op Profit	$ 193.03			
2014	Revenue	$ 352.55			
	Expense	$ 133.84			
	Investment	$ 30.00		$ 30.00	
	Net Op Profit	$ 218.70			
2015	Revenue	$ 387.80			
	Expense	$ 140.54			
	Investment	$ 30.00		$ 30.00	
	Net Op Profit	$ 247.27			

Baggage and Cargo Systems	Customer Service Practices	Gate and Hub Processes	Salary and Benefits Practices	Employee Flexibility and Retention	Similarity in Operating Philosophies
Adopt Best Practices	Adopt Best Practices	Adopt Best Practices	Develop Consistent Salary and Benefit Practices	Adopt Best Practices	Develop Consistent Operating Philosophies
	$ 10.00	$ 6.00	$ 20.00	$ 2.00	$ 8.00
$ 10.00					
	$ 4.00	$ 2.00			
$ 5.00					

Table 10.17 Discounted Cash Flow with Increased Expenses

	Prediction Year for Company A	New Company 2011	New Company 2012	New Company 2013	New Company 2014	New Company 2015
1	Net Operating Profit by Year (in millions)	$ 48.16	$ 152.96	$ 193.03	$ 218.70	$ 247.27
2	Estimated Amortization	$ 15.00	$ 15.00	$ 17.00	$ 19.00	$ 22.00
3	Operating Earnings Before Interest, Taxes, and Amortization (EBITA)	$ 63.16	$ 167.96	$ 210.03	$ 237.70	$ 269.27
4	Taxes on EBITA (35%)	$ 22.11	$ 58.79	$ 73.51	$ 83.20	$ 94.24
5	Changes in Deferred Taxes	$ (25.00)	$ (23.00)	$ (19.00)	$ (22.00)	$ (22.00)
6	Net Operating Profit Less Accumulated Taxes (NOPLAT)	$ 16.05	$ 86.17	$ 117.52	$ 132.51	$ 153.02
7	Net Investment	$ (48.00)	$ (63.00)	$ (45.00)	$ (30.00)	$ (30.00)
8	Free Cash Flow	$ (31.95)	$ 23.17	$ 72.52	$ 102.51	$ 123.02
9	Weighted Average Cost of Capital (WACC)	$ 0.05	$ 0.05	$ 0.05	$ 0.05	$ 0.05
10	Present Value of Cash Flows	$ (31.95)	$ 22.07	$ 65.78	$ 88.55	$ 101.21
11	**Total Present Value of Cash Flows in 5-Year Planning Horizon**	**$245.66**				

Table 10.18 Discounted Cash Flow with Increased Fleet Costs

	Prediction Year for Company A	**New Company 2011**	**New Company 2012**	**New Company 2013**	**New Company 2014**	**New Company 2015**
1	Net Operating Profit by Year (in millions)	$ 48.16	$ 152.96	$ 193.03	$ 218.70	$ 247.27
2	Estimated Amortization	$ 15.00	$ 15.00	$ 17.00	$ 19.00	$ 22.00
3	Operating Earnings Before Interest, Taxes, and Amortization (EBITA)	$ 63.16	$ 167.96	$ 210.03	$ 237.70	$ 269.27
4	Taxes on EBITA (35%)	$ 22.11	$ 58.79	$ 73.51	$ 83.20	$ 94.24
5	Changes in Deferred Taxes	$ (25.00)	$ (23.00)	$ (19.00)	$ (22.00)	$ (22.00)
6	Net Operating Profit Less Accumulated Taxes (NOPLAT)	$ 16.05	$ 86.17	$ 117.52	$ 132.51	$ 153.02
7	Net Investment	$ (63.00)	$ (88.00)	$ (67.25)	$ (45.00)	$ (45.00)
8	Free Cash Flow	$ (46.95)	$ (1.83)	$ 50.27	$ 87.51	$ 108.02
9	Weighted Average Cost of Capital (WACC)	$ 0.05	$ 0.05	$ 0.05	$ 0.05	$ 0.05
10	Present Value of Cash Flows	$ (46.95)	$ (1.74)	$ 45.59	$ 75.59	$ 88.87
11	**Total Present Value of Cash Flows in 5-Year Planning Horizon**	**$161.37**				

10.9 Summary

This case study provides one approach to analyzing the impacts and viability of merging two regional airlines.

The following is a summary of the key analyses for the merger specific application of the methodology:

- **Define the Objectives**—A common set of objectives are agreed upon by both companies and are weighted by the executives.

- **Developing Decision Criteria and Metrics**—Publicly available airline industry metrics make up the framework of the decision criteria that quantify and measure the accomplishment of the objectives.

- **Explore the Environment**—The integrated corporate planning activities are performed for the individual companies and the merged company to identify areas to focus efforts for a successful merger. The benchmarking and variability analysis is done using historical data and the coefficient of variation to analyze variability with a common statistical measure to indicate areas for focus and improvement. The functions of Finance, Marketing/Sales, and Corporate Strategy were identified as key focal areas while maintaining performance characteristics in the other functions.

- **Explore the Scope of the Problem and Its Importance**—Operational areas are identified in relationship to the decision criteria to focus on operational integration activities, identify the similarities and differences between the companies, identify an integration strategy, and develop projections of future financial metrics.

- **Data Mining and Statistical Analysis**—Revenues, expenses, investments, and net operating profits are projected from the operational impacts identified by exploring the scope of the problem.

- **Solve the Problem and Measure the Results**—The financial metrics and trends are developed from the operational impacts. A discounted cash flow is generated to determine the impacts of the merger on the overall business value.

- **Evaluate the Results and Do Sensitivity Analysis**—Financial assumptions are tested, and an alternative discounted cash flow is generated. Sensitivity analysis should be performed to gain confidence in the decisions, the assumptions, and the financial outcome of the merger.

This approach shows the steps involved to determine the objectives of the merger, develop the decision criteria and performance metrics analyzed in the study, and assess the performance levels of the two companies. The interactions between the various functional areas at their different performance levels are analyzed to determine key areas of focus in the merger activities. Operational impacts and financial ramifications of the merger requirements and actions are developed, and an overall assessment of the resulting company valuation is performed. The sensitivities associated with the decisions are then tested. The methods presented provide an overall view of different key components that should be analyzed in a merger activity and provide a well-rounded view of the potential success of the merger. The approach demonstrated for the airline merger can also be utilized in other integration activities within a company such as integrating product lines in manufacturing, consolidating functions, and others.

A

Overview of Methodologies

A.1 Decision Methodologies

This appendix provides an introductory survey of tools and methodologies that can be quite valuable in modeling in the decision-making environment. At this point in the process, the objectives have been identified, the metrics have been established, and the problem has been structured. The individuals developing the decision model should now look at the types of methodologies available to determine which approach best suits the problem at hand. A basic knowledge of the methodologies presented in this appendix is useful to identify those that have potential use in the model. You can perform a more detailed analysis by selecting a specific methodology with the best fit to model the problem.

Numerous books have been written about each of the types of methodologies listed in the book. The intention here is not to describe these in detail but to present some easily applied techniques that you can use in the decision-modeling process. Methodologies are presented in the following major categories: multiple criteria decision making; multiple objective decision making; artificial intelligence; statistical analysis; forecasting; expert opinion; fuzzy logic; and simulation.

A.2 Multiple Criteria Decision Making

Decisions that rank alternatives based on several criteria measured with subjective and objective data are best modeled by Multiple Criteria Decision Making methodologies. Subjective data is typically forward-looking as compared to objective data, which is historical. If some objective or historical data is readily available, this can be analyzed with statistics and used along with the subjective data that is analyzed with expert systems and used as input to the model. Numerous methods exist and can be applied to Multiple Criteria Decision Making models such as Simple Additive Weights (SAW) or the Technique for Order Preference by Similarity to Ideal Solution (TOPSIS), which are discussed later. These two methods are easiest to apply and easiest to understand.

Examples of Multiple Criteria Decision Making models may include the following:

- Selection of executives for promotion or retirement based on performance, evaluation criteria, and need of the organization
- Ranking critical items for the military based on their contributions to operation plans, readiness, sustainability, and availability
- Selecting products to keep or delete in a product line based on sales volume, future potential sales, strategic importance, and their impact on operations

If the time frame for the decision to be made is longer, you can use more sophisticated models to solve the problem. Based on the business conditions, the availability of data, the condition of data, the number of objectives of key decision makers, and the goals of the organization, you can use a number of methods when developing the model.

The following chart shows a number of Multiple Criteria Decision Making Methods that you can use to develop decision models (see Figure A.1). See the reference Hwang, et al for a discussion of these models. We have identified the easiest to use and easiest to understand that we normally use. These are Simple Additive Weights and TOPSIS for ranking and Successive Proportional Additive Numeration (SPAN) for expert group consensus as well as Brainstorming and Brainwriting for idea generation.

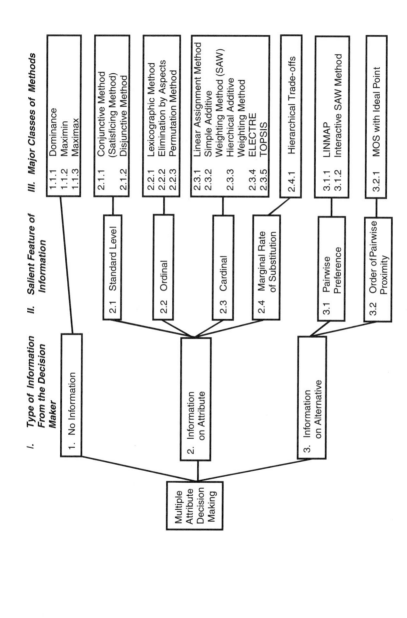

Figure A.1 A Taxonomy of Methods for Multiple Attribute Decision Making

A.3 Multiple Objective Decision Making

If the questions to be answered by the model involve the allocation of resources subject to constraints, you can apply a single objective or multiple objective optimization model to the problem. You can model a trade-off of objectives with Multiple Objective Decision Making in situations in which decisions involve several conflicting goals. Numerous methods exist to solve these problems. Examples of Multiple Objective Decision Making include the determination of the strategies for the U.S. negotiating team in Geneva where the objective is to maximize the U.S. total strategic capability and instantaneous strategic capability, subject to arms control and force structures constraints. The determination of a corporation's strategies and goals include long- and short-term goals, such as maximizing profit, while investing in research and development (R&D) and ensuring an adequate cash flow.

Few of the Multiple Objective methods, though, enable a true trade-off of objectives, and the biases associated with these methods must be understood prior to their application as part of the solution methodology. Also, depending on the linearity of the objective functions and constraints, you may need to apply nonlinear programming. The selection of the optimization model type, a single or multiple objective, linear or nonlinear method, is dependent on the environment modeled and the availability of data to support the model. The ability to generate an optimal solution representative of the "real world" is based upon developing a good representation of the problem at hand.

Figure A.2 shows a number of Multiple Objective Decision Making Methods that you can use to develop decision models. The specific method used to combine objectives into one of the standard linear or nonlinear algorithms is presented by C.L. Hwang and other references in the "References" section.

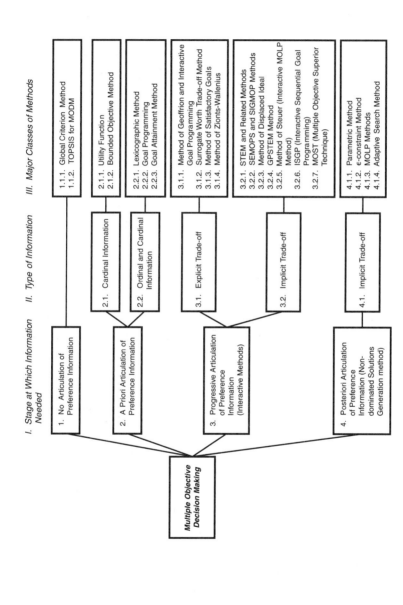

Figure A.2 A Taxonomy of Methods for Multiple Objective Decision Making

A.4 Artificial Intelligence

Numerous methodologies and techniques are available in the area of artificial intelligence (AI) that you can use to build decision models. Many software packages exist making it easy to develop these technologies into the framework of a model. Use AI technologies to model various activities and decisions within an organization, which data and information existing in an organization support. Neural Networks are a data-driven AI technology that you can use to generate an answer that is normally better by adjusting parameters than traditional methods of regression.

Expert systems are one of the most widely used forms of AI, and you can model a problem with many complex components using an expert system. This may include using a number of the different types of rule-based or object-oriented software packages to capture the decision rules and decision logic modeled. Capturing and coding decision rules within standard software packages can also be considered an expert system. A key in applying various expert systems is to not allow the expert system to become the objective of the effort. Many times the novelty of the expert system software and computational process overrides the actual purpose of the system or model developed. You need to maintain the focus of the actual goals and objectives of the problem modeled when applying an expert system to a given problem.

Fuzzy logic can also be considered AI. Fuzzy logic is especially beneficial in translating real-world representations of information into data that you can use in decision-model applications.

Genetic Algorithms rely on the concept of the "survival of the fittest." Therefore, when you use Genetic Algorithms, the best solutions are kept, and the worst solutions are eliminated based on testing the various possible solutions. Genetic Algorithms have gained popularity in use in stock market forecasting applications.

Neural Networks provide the capability for a system to learn from the data presented to the model. If sufficient amounts of data are available historically and on an on-going basis, a Neural Network can be beneficial in predicting the outcome of various events. Certain types of Neural Networks are statistically based, that is, the General Regression Neural Network (GRNN), which also can provide statistical explanation for the results.

Object-oriented programming (OOP) can also be considered an expert system. OOP involves encapsulating data for an object into its own individual unit. Parent-child relationships between objects can then be established to minimize the need to redefine characteristics of new or similar units. OOP represents more of a programming approach or philosophy used to represent a computing environment. Many off-the-shelf software packages support this type of computing approach.

Table A.1 shows a list of some of the more widely used AI technologies and some of their basic components.

A Neural Network is an AI technology inspired by studies of the brain and nervous system. A network accepts several inputs, performs a series of operations on these inputs, and produces one or more outputs. The network accomplishes this by recognizing patterns in the data sets and using these to adjust internal weights and parameters. A structured network can classify new patterns or make forecasts and predictions based on the evolving patterns in the data.

The Neural Network, especially the GRNN, provides the capability to predict future activities based on past activities by making parameter adjustments reflecting a constantly changing data environment. The GRNN also provides statistics similar to those produced in a Multiple Regression Analysis, which can make the Neural Network explainable to others from a statistical perspective. Other popular processing approaches or architectures such as Backpropagation and a polynomial network (Group Method of Data Handling) can be used to develop a Neural Network for a decision model.

A Neural Network provides the capability to incorporate up-to-date data from a variety of sources in the predictions, thus reflecting changes in operating characteristics of the business environment. This technology can be integrated into various system applications and easily operated by the user to provide a new type of analysis capability not currently used in the business environment.

Table A.1 Artificial Intelligence Methods

Technology	Components	Applications	Advantages	Disadvantages
Expert Systems Programs designed to model problem-solving capabilities of a human expert	Knowledge acquisition subsystem Knowledge base Inference engine Working memory User interface Explanation subsystem	Interpretation Prediction Diagnosis	Declarative information Naturally user friendly Explanation capabilities	Inflexible Information acquisition difficult
Fuzzy Logic Multivalued logic which enables intermediate values to be considered in problem solving	Degrees of truth falling between the range [0.0..1.0] with 0.0 meaning false and 1.0 meaning true	Linear control Nonlinear control Pattern recognition Expert system	Uses linguistic variables Easy knowledge acquisition and representation	Models difficult to create More fine tuning necessary
Genetic Algorithms Optimization algorithms in which competing solutions to a problem evolve until the best solutions are obtained	Initialization stage Evaluation and selection stage Crossover operations Mutation operation	Stock market forecasting Expert systems Fault diagnosis	Adaptable to diverse problems Solve large, intricate problems	Heavy computational requirements
Neural Networks Form of computing that models nervous system learning; mathematical structures with the capability to learn	Layers of processing elements Defined mathematical structures Defined inputs/outputs	Pattern recognition Classification Market forecasting	Good at identifying trends Capable of sorting complex data Learning capability	Lack of explanation capability Much time needed to train system
Object-Oriented Programming Approach that uses encapsulation of "packaging" in the process to design and build software.	Objects Encapsulation Subtyping Inheritance Design process/program methodology	Used as programming tool	Greater flexibility Reusable components, that is, menus	Objects may not be distinct Difficult with complex object interactions

A.5 Group Decision Making

The goal of Group Decision Making is to get a group consensus and determine the objectives that most satisfy the group overall while balancing the conflicting goals and objectives. These objectives can and do change over time and change with a different makeup of the group. You can apply numerous methods in Group Decision Making, but the simplest techniques are SPAN, Nominal Group Technique, Brainstorming, and Brainwriting. Each can be used to gain a group consensus of goals and objectives. You can apply different methods for Group Decision Making based on the expertise, dominance, and political nature of the various decision makers involved in the process. If, however, the group cannot agree somewhat on the objectives, there is no point in continuing the effort. All key decision makers must agree in general as to the goals and objectives to be accomplished; otherwise, there is no point to continue the model development effort.

You can also use Group Decision Making when subjective data about the future is the primary data available to support and develop a model. Because it is hard to easily look into the future, sometimes the one resource to get an estimate of future events is to poll experts in the field. Thus the methodologies suggested facilitate obtaining a weighted group consensus on future events. This is in comparison to a future forecast of events generated from past statistical data. The basic assumption of these models is that the future will behave as it has in the past. In the current business environment, this is seldom true, and no historical data is available. Group Decision Making is also useful when the problem is complex and difficult to define. The "gut feel" of experts can provide good information to support a model when no other data is available. The time frame for the decision can dictate the type of model and the type of data that can be gathered for use in the model. If the model must be developed quickly, the objectives identified in the Group Decision Making Process can be incorporated into a Multiple Criteria Decision Making model discussed later, which can use both objective and subjective data. Typically Multiple Criteria Decision Making models are less complex, thus less time-consuming, and are based on ranking alternatives.

A.6 Statistical Analysis

You can review these concepts in detail in various statistics texts and production planning books. Many more sophisticated techniques are available. The purpose of listing the topics here is to highlight some readily known basic techniques, which are easily understood and applied, that you can use to gain a great deal of understanding of the data for the model. We are not presenting a study of statistics but are simply pointing out concepts useful in data analyses. These functions are readily available in spreadsheets and databases such as MS Excel and MS Access.

A.6.1 Standard Statistics

Following are some standard statistics that you can use to analyze current and historical data. These statistical functions are readily available in Microsoft Excel or Microsoft Access.

- **Mean**—The arithmetic mean or average of the data set.
- **Low**—The lowest value in the data set.
- **High**—The highest value in the data set.
- **Median**—The value that represents the middle of the data set when ordered. If there are not equal occurrences above and below the median, an average of the two middle values is taken.
- **Mode**—The most frequent value in the set of data.
- **Standard deviation**—The measure of dispersion of a frequency distribution that is the square root of the arithmetic mean of the squares of the deviation of each of the class frequencies from the arithmetic mean of the frequency distribution.
- **Variance**—The measure of dispersion of a frequency distribution that is the arithmetic mean of the squares of the deviation of each of the class frequencies from the arithmetic mean of the frequency distribution.

A.6.2 Histogram

A histogram is a representation of a frequency distribution divided by classes of data and plotted according to the frequency of the occurrence for each of the classes of data against another axis, for example, time, color, and so on. This plot can be performed using a line graph or with bar graphs, whichever is the typical representation for this data. Most likely, the data used to develop the histogram will be represented by integer groupings, that is, 1 day or 2 days, or can be grouped into ranges of data such as 0–3 days, 4–6 days, and so on.

A.6.3 Frequency Distribution for the Data Set by Deciles

This is similar to the development of the histogram; however, the frequency distribution would be divided into 10 equal classes of data such that each class contains the same number of individual data points. Ranges or averages associated with each of the classes of data would display on the plot of the information and can also display in tabular form.

A.6.4 Determining Safety Stock and Production Variability

If the modeling environment requires the determination of safety stock to cover the variability in a process, statistical analysis is useful for this purpose. The ability for a company to have product on hand, or make an informed decision not to have product on hand, directly impacts the end-user level of satisfaction of the service of the company. Costs, production, and capacity considerations may impact an organization's ability to meet safety stock requirements. However, the ability or inability to supply product to customers directly impacts the bottom line of a company's operations in a number of ways. Using statistical analysis gives you insight on how to account for this variability.

You can translate this statistical analysis of the variability of the process into safety stock levels maintained so that a supplier has a predetermined amount of product on hand regardless of the demand and production variability. For example, you can set safety stock levels so that a product is on hand 95% of the time, based on the statistical analysis of the variability of the process. This would mean that you would run out of a given product only five times out of one hundred or 5% of the time, based on the average sales and the average amount of product maintained in inventory. Often, different products have different safety stock requirements. Management may state that the flagship products of a company should never be out of stock. You would set the safety stock levels for these products high in this case. However, when setting safety stock levels, you must also consider the amount of storage space required and cost for the product in inventory as well as the variability in production and sales.

A.7 Forecasting

You can use a number of different forecasting techniques to predict future occurrences based on historical data. The most common of the techniques are moving averages, exponential smoothing, and multiple regression analysis. These techniques are discussed in much more detail in a number of statistics books.

A.7.1 Moving Averages

A moving average is a forecast for a future occurrence of an activity based on the most recent occurrences of the activity. The simple moving average is the arithmetic mean of the n most recent observations. Following are several characteristics of this model. First, equal weights are assigned to the most recent n observations. Second, each new estimate is computed by adding the new data point and discarding the oldest data point for the previous nth period. Thus, each new estimate is an updated version of the preceding estimate. Third, the rate of response of the moving average to changes in the underlying data pattern depends upon the number of periods included in the moving average. In general, the more periods included in the computation, the less sensitive it will be to changes in the pattern of the data. Conversely, a small value of n leads to a moving average that responds relatively rapidly to changes and may have much more variability.

A.7.2 Weighted Moving Averages

Creating weighted moving average forecasts is based on utilizing the concepts of the moving average; however, possibly weighting the most recent observations more in the forecasting process. The weighted moving average enables the observations to be weighted such that more importance can be attached to the more recent observations. The weights should sum to one.

A.7.3 Exponential Smoothing

In the exponential smoothing method, new forecasts are derived by adjusting forecasts made for previous periods by considering its forecast error. In this way, the forecaster can continually revise the forecast based on past experience. The model has the advantage of a weighted moving average method, in that more recent observations are assigned larger weights. It reacts faster than the moving average model to changes in the variability of the data. Single exponential smoothing is a procedure in which the forecast for the next period equals the forecast for the prior period adjusted by an amount proportional to the most recent forecast. Double exponential smoothing may also be used to address trends in the data.

The smoothing constant α must be determined judgmentally, depending on the sensitivity of response required by the model. The smaller the value of α, the slower the response. Larger values of α cause increasingly quicker reactions in the smoothed (forecast) value. Another difficulty with this method occurs when trying to forecast more than one period ahead. Therefore, this method is designed for and is best to use to forecast only one period ahead.

A.7.4 Regression Analysis

This approach to forecasting involves determining the relationships between the dependent and independent variables and representing this relationship in a regression equation. The results of this statistical analysis can be shown in an equation, in tables, or by plotting the regression line for the data set. Regression is a functional relationship between two or more correlated variables that is often empirically determined from data and is used to predict values of one variable when given values of the others.

Regression equations can be used to predict future requirements or activities based on variables input into the regression equations. For example, the variables or drivers can be utilized to predict future workloads based on the past relationships between the workload drivers and the resulting work performed.

You can also use stepwise regression to develop a multiple variable equation for forecasting. Do this by adding new variables to the equation and checking to see if the new equation provides a better forecast; for example, reduce the variability around the forecasted value. Stepwise regression uses a statistical test called the F-Test to identify this subset of variables. The F-Test is a test that validates whether the variance is reduced significantly around the forecasted value. In the regression analysis, the F-Test would test whether the variance of the variables used in the regression equation is equal to or less than the variance in the original data. Based on the F-Test, variables are either entered if they reduce the variance or removed if they don't from the subset one at a time until the optimal combination of variables is found. The resulting subset is the minimal best set of variables that significantly reduce the variance and are the most accurate in the predictions or forecasts.

A.8 Expert Opinion

Individuals that have been with an organization for long periods of time generally have a great deal of experience about the organization and possess knowledge that can be captured and used for model building. This type of data or opinion is not typically maintained in a database. Many times this data is not easily incorporated into a decision process. Expert Opinion can be captured from individuals in a variety of ways. Some examples of how Expert Opinion can be captured include the following:

- Judgment and opinion of project success
- Opinions of which are the key areas for strategic planning
- New product potential
- Establishing organizational goals and objectives
- Ranking available options
- Rating the decision criteria used to assess projects
- Providing assessment of future projections

Expert Opinion is often overlooked in the decision modeling process. Expert Opinion integrates the knowledge of an individual and where his or her sum total of experience determines his or her perception of the future. With a structured approach, this knowledge can be quantified, captured, and integrated into the decision process. Much valuable information can be captured from individuals with in-depth knowledge about an organization and if not obtained this way would not be used to help make decisions. Expert Opinion is forward looking whereas statistical data, on the other hand, is solely based on backward or historical observations. The assumption in statistical models is that the future will be the same as the past, whereas Expert Opinion can capture what will happen in the future in a fast-changing business climate in the future.

A.9 Fuzzy Logic

Fuzzy logic is an innovative technology that you can use in decision modeling, which enables the model to use imprecise data or data not strictly defined. Boolean or classical yes/no types of answers are not necessary with fuzzy logic. Fuzzy logic enables information to be expressed in more real-world terms or terms that have more blurred boundaries. For example, you can use fuzzy logic to classify the height of women. If 5'4" to 5'8" is average height for women, someone that is 5' 8 1/32" might still be considered average height. You could also rate the temperature outside with terms like "a little chilly," "a nice day," "a scorcher," or "a day I can fry eggs on the black top." Fuzzy logic "brings home" the use of such data in a decision model.

Fuzzy logic provides an innovative and less structured approach to the analysis and integration of data and the relationship between data and decision logic. Fuzzy logic has the capability to significantly lower the analysis and design requirements for an expert system by decreasing the size and complexity of the rule set with no impact on the quality of the answer. In many situations, fuzzy logic can actually increase the effectiveness of the mathematical model by enabling it to more accurately model imprecise information. Its use on everything from camcorders to weapon systems serves to further enhance its value in the decision-making process.

It differs from statistics in that statistics provides point estimates, whereas fuzzy logic would put confidence intervals around the estimates. When you are not certain and make a subjective estimate, you might state the estimate as a range of values. That is, you would have a confidence of 30 percent that the actual value would fall in the interval 8 to 10, whereas you would have a confidence of 80 percent that the value would fall in the interval 5 to 9.

A.10 Simulation

Most Multiple Objective models are measured in discrete time units. Simulation models, however, model transactions over a period of time. Typically, in simulation models, rules of thumb, ranges of values, and Boolean decisions can be included or imbedded into simulation models via expert systems to develop a realistic representation of a real-world environment. Applying simulation and expert system techniques enables you to model complex situations without connectivity. Computer software packages such as ARENA, GPSS, SIMAN, and SLAM are available to develop simulation models. Simulation enables decision makers to approximate an environment and explore parameters to develop a "better solution." Where there is no guarantee in simulation of an optimal solution, you can achieve a better solution with a realistic simulation model of the environment by exploring a number of scenarios varying business constraints, operating rules, and costs.

B

Detailed Methodologies

B.1 Nominal Group Technique (NGT)

This methodology provides a systematic approach to develop a set of goals for the group, while incorporating input from all the group members. NGT combines elements of Brainwriting, Brainstorming, and voting techniques to produce a method that has been used in a variety of organizations for idea-generation. Meeting setup consists of assembling a group of five to nine experts representing the customer requirements and program management. Preferably, the room setup should avoid interference between attendees. A flip chart to record ideas should be visible to all participants. The materials required for the meeting are a flip chart, 3 x 5 cards, tape, pens, paper, and pencils.

Step 1. **Introducing the meeting**—A quick statement should be made by the program manager stating the purpose of the meeting. This process establishes the overall goals and decision criteria to support each of the objectives.

Step 2. **Silently generating ideas in writing**—Have each of the participants write down objectives/criteria on paper without discussion with anyone else at the table. Allow 10 to 15 minutes for the effort.

Step 3. **Round-robin recording of ideas**—Record the objectives/criteria on a flip chart or chalkboard visible to the group. Go around the table and ask for one idea from one member at a time, writing down the ideas on the flip chart.

Step 4. General discussion for clarification—Clarify or elaborate on ideas and add new ideas to list as they arise.

Step 5. Preliminary vote on item importance—This consists of the following steps:

   a. Have participants select between five to nine priority items.

   b. Place each priority idea on a separate 3 x 5 card.

   c. Rank-order or rate the selected priority ideas by assigning, for example, a 7 to the highest priority item and a 1 to the lowest priority item, if 7 items were selected from the list.

   d. Collect cards and shuffle the cards to maintain anonymity of votes.

   e. Tally votes and record results on the flip chart in front of the group.

Step 6. Discussion of preliminary vote—Discuss results of votes; clarify inconsistent voting patterns, rediscuss ideas that are perceived as receiving too many or too few votes. Modify ideas accordingly.

Step 7. Final vote—Repeat step 5 to develop a final vote.

B.2 Normalized Direct Weighting

This approach is a simple, intuitive weighting approach in which each objective or criteria is given a score and the score is then normalized so that the sum of the normalized weights totals to 100 percent. Following is an example of weighting of sample objectives utilizing this approach. Each objective is assigned a score between 1 and 10. From this, a percentage of the total is calculated to represent the normalized weight.

	Score	Calculation	Normalized Weight
COST	10	10/50	20.0%
RISK	8	8/50	16.0%
PERFORMANCE	10	10/50	20.0%
RELIABILITY	6	6/50	12.0%
MAINTAINABILITY	5	5/50	10.0%
PRODUCIBILITY	6	6/50	12.0%
ENVIRONMENTAL IMPACT	5	5/50	10.0%
SUM	50		

B.3 Analytical Hierarchy Process (Eigenvector Method)

This approach is based on the decision maker assigning a comparative value of importance for each of the criteria. The criteria are compared against each other, and a relative degree of importance is assigned in the comparison. A rating scale ranging from 1 to 9 is used to assign the degree of importance one criteria has over the other. An example is shown here where the importance of decision criteria A is more important than decision criteria B and the degree of that importance is valued at 7—Demonstrated importance.

Decision Criteria A	compared to	Decision Criteria B
1		Equal importance
2		
3		Weak importance
4		
5		Essential or strong importance
6		
7		Demonstrated importance
8		
9		Absolute importance

The comparison process is stored in a matrix, including the direct comparisons and their reciprocal value, and the normalized Eigenvector value is then computed. This method enables the user to achieve a more finely tuned weighting but takes more time to accomplish based on the number of criteria. The more criteria there are, the greater the number of pairs that need to be compared and evaluated. There is a limited number of criteria and alternatives, such as five or six, that should be considered using this method because of the time required for the evaluation and the consistency between the paired comparisons.

Mathematical Calculations

Refer to C.L. Hwang's book, *Multiple Attribute Decision Making*, for a description of the mathematical calculations.

B.4 Simple Additive Weighting Method

Description

The Simple Additive Weighting method (SAW) is probably the best known and widely used method of Multiple Attribute Decision Making. To each of the attributes in SAW the decision maker assigns importance weights, which become the coefficients of the variables. These weight coefficients need to be normalized. To reflect the decision maker's marginal worth assessments within attributes, the decision maker also makes a numerical scaling of intra-attribute values. The decision maker can then obtain a total score for each alternative simply by multiplying the scale rating for each attribute value by the importance weight assigned to the attribute and then summing these products over all attributes. After the total scores are computed for each alternative, the alternative with the highest score (the highest weighted average) is the one prescribed to the decision maker.

Mathematical Computations

Mathematically, a simple additive weighting method can be stated as follows: Suppose the decision maker assigns a set of importance weights to the attributes, $w = \{w_1, w_2, \ldots w_n\}$. The most preferred alternative A*, is selected such that

$$A^* = \left\{ A_i \middle| \max_i \frac{\sum_{j=1}^{n} w_j x_{ij}}{\sum_{j=1}^{n} w_j} \right\}$$

where x_{ij} is the outcome of the ith alternative about the jth attribute with numerically comparable scale. Usually the weights are normalized so that

$$\sum_{j=1}^{n} w_j = 1.$$

Precautions

There are some precautions that are important when developing decision models.

1. Scaling of criteria value can greatly influence the impact of a single criteria and thus the ranking. To avoid this problem, all values within a criteria are normalized.

2. Independence—Care should be taken so that all the criteria are independent, thus avoiding overweighing the effects of a criteria.

B.5 Borda's Function

This is a group decision making method that is a social choice function based on a preferential rating system used to arrive at a consensus ranking from the participants. This is a rank order method in which each of the candidates are ranked by each of the voters. The score is then determined by adding each rank score for each candidates. In this example, the score is used to determine a set of weights for the criteria.

The method Borda proposes is the rank-order method. With candidates in A, assign marks of m-1, m-2,...,1,0 to the first ranked, second ranked, ..., last ranked candidate for each individual. Then determine the Borda score for each candidate as the sum of the individual marks for that candidate. Then the candidate with the highest Borda score is declared the winner. The Borda score of a candidate x is equivalent to the sum of the number of individuals that have x preferred to y for all y ∈ A|{x}.

A modified Borda method is proposed here, which is the same used by the weekly national wire service poll of the top 20 best college basketball teams in the United States. Approximately 60 sports writers and broadcasters each assign 20 points, 19 points, ..., 2 points, 1 point, to his/her first ranked, second ranked, ..., 19th ranked, and 20th ranked college teams, respectively. These 20 teams are selected from more than 100 college teams. The final choice of the top 20 teams is ranked in the order of each team's total points received from the 60 voters.

B.6 TOPSIS

The Technique for Order Preference by Similarity to Ideal Solution (TOPSIS) is a Multiple Attribute Decision Making problem with a number of alternatives evaluated by a number of attributes. The TOPSIS methodology is viewed as a geometric system with m points in the n-dimensional space. TOPSIS is based on the concept that the chosen alternative should have the shortest distance to the best possible attribute assessment values (positive-ideal solution) and have the longest distance from the worst possible assessment values (negative-ideal solution) for each of the alternatives.

An ideal solution is defined as a collection of ideal levels for the attribute levels. An ideal solution, however, is ideal and usually not attainable. The TOPSIS methodology uses concepts to come closest to the best possible answers and farthest from the worst possible answers. The positive-ideal and negative-ideal solutions are used in this methodology to find the best feasible alternative given the options and evaluations available.

Formally, the positive-ideal solution is denoted as

$$A^* = (x^*_1, ..., x^*_j,...,x^*_n)$$

where x^*_j is the best value for the jth attribute among all the available alternatives.

The negative ideal solution is denoted as

$$A^- = (x^-_1, ..., x^-_j,...,x^-_n)$$

where x^-_j is the worst value for the jth attribute among all the available alternatives.

TOPSIS defines an index called similarity (or relative closeness) to the positive-ideal solution by combining the proximity to the positive-ideal solutions and the remoteness from the negative-ideal solution. Then the method chooses an alternative with the maximum similarity to the positive-ideal solution. TOPSIS assumes that each attribute takes either monotonically increasing or monotonically decreasing utility. That is, the larger the attribute outcome, the greater the preference for benefit attributes and the less the preference for cost attributes.

The method presented is a series of successive steps:

Step 1. Calculate normalized ratings. The vector normalizations is used for computing r_{ij}, which is given as

$$r_{ij} = \frac{x_{ij}}{\sqrt{\sum_{i=1}^{m} x^2_{ij}}} \text{ where } i = 1,...,m; j = 1,..., n$$

Step 2. Calculate weighted normalized ratings. The weighted normalized value is calculated as

$$v_{ij} = w_j r_{ij}, i = 1, ..., m; j = 1, ..., n$$

where w_j is the weight of the jth attribute.

Step 3. **Identify positive-ideal and negative-ideal solutions**. The A^* and A^- are defined in terms of the weighted normalized values:

$$A^* = \{v^*_1, \ldots, v^*_j, \ldots, v^*_n\}$$

$$= \{(\max_i v_{ij} | j \in J_1), (\min_i v_{ij} | j \in J_2) | i = 1, \ldots, m\}$$

$$A^- = \{v^-_1, \ldots, v^-_j, \ldots, v^-_n\}$$

$$= \{(\min_i v_{ij} | j \in J_1), \{(\max_i v_{ij} | j \in J_2) | i = 1, \ldots, m\}$$

where J_1 is a set of benefit attributes, and J_2 is a set of cost attributes.

Step 4. **Calculate separation measures**. The separation (distance) between alternatives can be measured by the n-dimensional Euclidean distance. The separation of each alternative from the positive-ideal solution, A^*, is then given by

$$S^* = \sqrt{\sum_{j=1}^{n} (v_{ij} - v^*_i)^2} \text{ where } i = 1, \ldots, m.$$

Similarly, the separation from the negative-ideal solution, A^-, is given by

$$S^-_i = \sqrt{\sum_{j=1}^{n} (v_{ij} - v^-_j)^2} \text{ where } i = 1, \ldots, m.$$

Step 5. **Calculate similarities to positive-ideal solution**.

$$C^*_i = S^-_i / (S^*_i + S^-_i), i = 1, \ldots, m.$$

Note that $0 \le C^*_i \le 1$, where $C^*_i = 0$ when $A_i = A^-$, and $C^*_i = 1$ when $A_i = A^*$.

Step 6. **Rank preference order**. Choose an alternative with the maximum C^*_i or rank alternatives according to C^*_i in descending order.

B.6.1 TOPSIS Sensitivity Analysis

The activities and results from Chapter 1, "Define the Objectives and Identify Metrics," provide a means to identify the key drivers associated with the assessment of technology development alternatives. You can perform sensitivity analysis on the current ranked list of technology alternatives to determine how much an alternative evaluation criteria must change to move an alternative up or down in the ranked list of projects. The importance weighting of the evaluation criteria and the evaluation scores for the alternatives drive the alternative scoring in terms meeting customer and organizational goals, as shown in the relative closeness generated by the TOPSIS methodology. Sensitivity analysis is useful in identifying the key drivers of the overall value of an alternative. The specific subcriteria evaluations for the alternatives provide the supporting detail to show why certain alternatives received the scores that they did and can be used to pinpoint potential areas for improvement and additional trades.

The methodology used to perform sensitivity analysis consists of testing each criteria for each alternatives to determine what the value would need to be to move the alternative up or down in rank. To determine the values of the criteria for the alternatives required to move the alternative up in rank, the criteria is incremented one increment closer to the positive-ideal solution. To determine the values of the criteria for the alternatives required to move the alternative down in rank, the criteria is incremented one increment closer to the negative-ideal solution. The ranking (TOPSIS) program is then run and the results are tested against the original ranking to determine if the change in this criteria value has moved the alternative up (or down) in the rank of the alternatives. The incrementing process continues until a value is determined that can move the criteria up (or down) in rank or the incrementing process reaches the positive-ideal (negative-ideal) solution. If the incrementing process reaches the positive-ideal (negative-ideal) solution and the alternative still does not move up (or down) in rank, it is then infeasible to change the specific criteria value to move the alternative up (or down) in rank. This is done for each of the criteria for all alternatives. Also the incrementing process is done on only one criteria value at a time, thus testing each criteria value independent of any other changes made to the other criteria values.

B.7 SPAN

This group consensus technique enables individuals of a committee to have different weights or votes on issues. The individuals are assigned equal quantities of votes, say 100, which are allocated between the options and the experts. Then, each of the experts are assigned a percentage of the votes allocated for the experts, and each of the options are assigned a percentage of the votes allocated for the options. The original votes are then distributed among the options based on the original distribution input by the decision maker.

The steps for using the SPAN technique follow:

Step 1. Each individual is allocated an original quota of points. Usually a parcel of 100 points is equally distributed among the participants.

Step 2. The individuals distribute their points among other individuals and options. Although the participants can be given complete freedom to determine the proportions, it is generally recommended that a small percentage be allocated to at least one of the options.

Step 3. Each individual allocates subparcels of points to either the other individuals and/or the options, that is, to establish the proportions they want. The values of proportions in steps 2 and 3 are fixed for subsequent cycles; then the new allocations should be similar to those used in the first cycle.

Step 4. Using a manual or computer program, the process continues through as many successive cycles as needed to distribute all the points among the options. The terminal point is reached when the cumulative final points among the options are equal or close to (say, less than 0.1 percent) the total number of original points. The parcels located at the options, unlike those located among individuals, will not be redistributed.

Step 5. The option with the greatest number of points is selected as the best alternative in cumulative final points.

Example:

Three members select one option from a set of two options. The example shown in Table B.1 shows the following.

1. Each individual is given a parcel of 100 points.

2. The individuals establish the proportions they want to use in allocating points to members and the options. For example, Table B.1, with fictional data tells us that member A in a three-person group allocated 76 percent to Option 1 and 24 percent to Option 2.

3. Based on the proportion assignments each individual allocates subparcels of points to either of the other individuals and/or the options. For example in Table B.1, member A directed 100 percent to individual B, and it is also known that he assigned 30 percent to members; therefore, this parcel has 30 points. He also assigned 70 points to options as a whole, which were split 76 percent (53.2 points) for Option 1 and 24 percent (16.8 points) for Option 2.

4. The cycle of calculations was to proceed to find the distributed option points. You can continue the procedure until the sum of the option points is almost exactly that of the original points, in this example, 300.

5. The final result is that Option 1 has received 158.4 cumulative final points versus 141.6 for Option 2. The two numbers sum to 300. Option 1 was selected as a better alternative.

Table B.1 Three Allocations of Percentages by Each Member

Target	Sender A	Sender B	Sender C
Members (A, B, and C)	30	60	80
Options (1 and 2)	70	40	20
Member A	0	95	0
Member B	100	0	100
Member C	0	5	0
Option 1	76	25	0
Option 2	24	75	100

B.8 Brainstorming

Brainstorming is an idea generation technique by which a group attempts to find a solution for a specific problem by assuming all the ideas spontaneously contributed by its members. Its strength is the creative collaboration by a group is better than an individual. The four basic rules to a brainstorming session are as follows:

1. Criticism is ruled out. This is the most important rule.
2. Free-wheeling is welcomed.
3. Quantity is wanted.
4. A combination of ideas and improvement on ideas is sought.

The brainstorming group consists of members, a leader, and a secretary. The leader should remind the members of the problem and the rules, and the secretary records the ideas. The group should consist of 6 to 12 people of equal status. The problem should be well defined with the participants aware of the problem one week in advance. The leader should record the suggestions on a visible medium to all participants and re-read the generated suggestions if necessary. The session should not last longer than 1 hour.

B.9 Brainwriting

Brainwriting is an idea generation technique, similar to brainstorming, which uses written ideas instead of verbal communication. The steps of the procedure follow:

1. There are four to eight participants with a group leader.
2. Each participant inputs one to four ideas about the problem.
3. Then each participant views five random ideas and adds one to two more.
4. The participants then continue to add new ideas to the system.
5. This process goes on for 30 to 40 minutes or until the group appears to have exhausted its ideas.
6. The ideas are then viewed or printed for later evaluation.

The brainwriting pool is deceptively simple and is also easy to learn and use.

Some advantages include the following:

1. All members of the group are working in parallel, instead of singularly in sequence.
2. Absence of verbal criticism creates free thinking and mild tension.
3. Every idea gets recorded and none are lost.
4. Reading what others write provides a continuing learning opportunity and a stimulus to thought.
5. Dominance by strong personalities is eliminated.
6. Premature closure is eliminated.

B.10 Moving Averages

A moving average is a forecast for a future occurrence of an activity based on the most recent occurrences of the activity. The simple moving average model is given by the formula

$$m_t = \frac{1}{n}\sum_{i=0}^{n-1} y_{t-i} = \frac{y_t + y_{t-1} + y_{t-2} + \ldots + y_{t-n+1}}{n} \qquad \{1\}$$

where

m_t = Moving average at time t

y_t = Actual value in period t

n = Number of terms included in the moving average

The simple moving average is the arithmetic mean of the n most recent observations.

For computational purposes, the simple moving average can be restated as

$$m_t = m_{t-1} + \frac{y_t - y_{t-n}}{n} \qquad \{2\}$$

Several characteristics of this model should be noted.

1. Equal weights are assigned to the most recent n observations.
2. Each new estimate of m_t is computed by adding the new data point and discarding the oldest data point for the previous nth period. Thus, each *new* estimate of m_t is an updated version of the preceding estimate.
3. The rate of response of the moving average to changes in the underlying data pattern depends upon the number of periods included in the moving average. In general, the more periods included in the computation, the less sensitive it will be to changes in the pattern of the data. Conversely, a small value of n leads to a moving average that responds relatively rapidly to changes and may have much more variability.

To compute forecasts for periods beyond the current period, t, equation (1) must be modified as follows:

$$\hat{y}_{t+1} = m_t = \frac{y_t + y_{t-1} + y_{t-2} + \ldots + y_{t-n+1}}{n} \qquad \{3\}$$

or

$$\hat{y}_{t+3} = \frac{\hat{y}_{t+2} + \hat{y}_{t+1} + y_t + y_{t-1} + \ldots + y_{t-n+3}}{n} \qquad \{4\}$$

where the ^'s refer to forecasted values.

Thus, the moving average for 3 periods in the future is computed using the moving average values for periods 1 and 2 in the future.

B.11 Weighted Moving Averages

Creating Weighted Moving Average forecasts are based on utilizing the concepts of the moving average, however, possibly weighting the most recent observations more in the forecasting process. The weighted moving average model is given by the formula:

$$m_t = \sum_{i=0}^{n-1} w_{n-i}\, y_{t-i} = w_n\, y_t + w_{n-1}\, y_{t-1} + \ldots + w_1\, y_{t-n+1}$$

$$\sum_{i=0}^{n-1} \text{where} \quad w_{n-i} = w_n + w_{n-1} + \ldots + w_1 = 1.$$

m_t = Weighted moving average at time t

y_t = Actual value in period t

n = Number of terms included in the moving average

w_t = Weight on observation for period t

The weighted moving average enables the observations to be weighted such that more importance can be attached to the more recent observations. The weights should sum to 1.

B.12 Exponential Smoothing

In the Exponential Smoothing method, new forecasts are derived by adjusting forecasts made for previous periods using its forecast error. In this way, the forecaster can continually revise the forecast based on past experience. The model has the advantage of a weighted moving average method, in that more recent observations are assigned larger weights. It reacts even faster than the moving average model to changes in the pattern of the data.

The formula for computing the single exponential smoothing value is

$$s_{t+1} = \alpha\, y_t + (1-\alpha)\, s_t \qquad \{1\}$$

where

s_{t+1} = Single exponential smoothing forecast for the next period

s_t = Single exponential smoothing forecast for the current period

y_t = Actual value in time period t

α = Smoothing constant ($0 < \alpha < 1$)

By rewriting s_t in another way as

$$s_{t+1} = s_t + \alpha(y_t - s_t) \qquad \{2\}$$

it can be seen that single exponential smoothing is a procedure in which the forecast for the next period equals the forecast for the prior period adjusted by an amount proportional to the most recent forecast error

$$e_t = y_t - s_t \qquad \{3\}$$

This illustrates how the current forecast error is used to modify the forecast for the next period.

The name "exponential smoothing" comes from the fact that s_t can be expressed as a *weighted average* with exponentially decreasing weights. To see how this is so, you can substitute the expression for s_t and s_{t-1}, in the original expression for s_{t+1}.

$$s_t = \alpha\, y_{t-1} + (1-\alpha)\, s_{t-1} \qquad \{4\}$$

$$s_{t-1} = \alpha\, y_{t-2} + (1-\alpha)\, s_{t-2} \qquad \{5\}$$

You can substitute equations {4} and {5} into the original expression for s_{t+1} as follows:

$$s_{t+1} = \alpha\, y_t + (1-\alpha)\,[\alpha\, y_{t-1} + (1-\alpha)\, s_{t-1}]$$
$$= \alpha\, y_t + \alpha\,(1-\alpha)\, y_{t-1} + \alpha\,(1-\alpha)^2\, y_{t-2} + (1-\alpha)^3\, s_{t-2} \qquad \{6\}$$

Substituting recursively for s_{t-2}, s_{t-3}, and so on, you obtain

$$s_{t+1} = \alpha\, y_t + \alpha\,(1-\alpha)\, y_{t-1} + \alpha\,(1-\alpha)^2\, y_{t-2} + \ldots$$
$$+ \alpha\,(1-\alpha)^{t-1}\, y_1 + (1-\alpha)^t\, s_0 \qquad \{7\}$$

or

$$s_{t+1} = \alpha \sum_{k=0}^{t-1}(1-\alpha)^k\, y_{t-k} + (1-\alpha)^t\, s_0 \qquad (0 < \alpha < 1) \qquad \{8\}$$

where

s_0 = initial estimate of the smoothed value

The initial estimate s_0 of the smoothed value can be estimated from historical data by using a simple average of the most recent observations. The receding equation shows that s_{t+1} is a weighted average of y_t, y_{t-1}, y_{t-2}, . . ., y_1 and the initial estimate of s_0. The coefficients of the observations

$$\alpha, \alpha(1-\alpha), \alpha(1-\alpha)^2, \ldots, \alpha(1-\alpha)^{t-1}$$

are the weights and measure the contribution each observation makes to the most recent estimate. The weights decrease geometrically with increasing k so that the most recent values of y_t are given the most weight. Values of y_t more distant in the past make successively smaller contributions to s_t.

The smoothing constant α must be determined judgmentally, depending on the sensitivity of response required by the model. The smaller the value of α, the slower the response. Larger values of α cause increasingly quicker reactions in the smoothed (forecast) value. Some text books recommend that α should lie somewhere between 0.01 and 0.30 or 0.40.

Another difficulty with this method occurs when trying to forecast more than one period ahead. Therefore, this method is designed for and is best to use to forecast only one period ahead. Also, an extension of this method is double exponential smoothing which can be used to address trends in the data.

B.13 Regression Analysis

This approach to forecasting involves determining the relationships between the dependent and independent variables and representing this relationship in a regression equation. The results of this statistical analysis can be shown in an equation, in tables, or by plotting the regression line for the data set. Regression is a functional relationship between two or more correlated variables that is often empirically determined from data and is used to predict values of one variable when given values of the others.

You can use regression equations to predict future requirements or activities based on variables input into the regression equations. For example, use the variables or drivers to predict future workloads based on the past relationships between the workload drivers and the resulting work performed.

The general form of the regression equations used in this analysis is shown here:

$$y = \sum_{i=1}^{n} a_i x_i + b,$$

where a_i is the coefficient of each input variable, x_i is the actual value of the input variable, and b is the intercept.

You can also use stepwise regression to develop multiple variable equation for forecasting. You can do this by adding new variables to the equation and checking to see if the new equation provides a better forecast, for example, reduces the variability around the forecasted value. Stepwise regression uses a statistical test called the F-Test to identify this subset of variables. The F-Test is a test that validates whether the variance is reduced around the forecasted value. In the regression analysis, the F-Test would test whether the variance of the variables used in the regression equation is equal to or less than the variance in the original data. Based on the F-Test, variables are either entered if they reduce the variance or removed if they don't from the subset one at a time until the optimal combination of variables is found. The resulting subset is the best set of variables that significantly reduce the variance and are the most accurate in the predictions or forecasts. Once you have your data in a spreadsheet such as MS Excel, you can utilize the built-in functions in MS Excel to perform the analysis.

References

Cassone, Deandra T. Dissertation: "A Process to Estimate the Value of a Company Using Operational Performance Metrics," Kansas State University, 2005.

Chen, Shu-Jen, and Ching-Lai Hwang in collaboration with Frank P. Hwang. "Fuzzy Multiple Attribute Decision Making," Springer-Verlag, New York, New York, 1992.

Hwang, Ching-Lai, and Masud, Abu Syed Md. "Multiple Objective Decision Making—Methods and Applications," Springer-Verlag, Berlin, Germany, 1979.

Hwang, Ching-Lai, and Ming-Jen Lin. "Group Decision Making Under Multiple Criteria," Springer-Verlag, Berlin, Germany, 1987.

Hwang, Ching-Lai, and K. Yoon. "Multiple Attribute Decision Making — Methods and Applications, A State-of-the-Art Survey," Springer-Verlag, Berlin, Germany, 1981.

Tillman, Frank A., and Deandra T. Cassone, "Integrated Business Decisions, Analyses and Strategies," Textbook self-published for use in courses at Kansas State University, College of Business Administration, MBA Program, 2002.

Wolter J. Fabrycky, and Benjamin S. Blanchard. *Life-Cycle Cost and Economic Analysis*, Prentice Hall, 1991.

Yoon, K. Paul, and Ching-Lai Hwang. "Multiple Attribute Decision Making—An Introduction, Series: Quantitative Applications in the Social Sciences," A Sage University Paper, 104, Thousand Oaks, CA: Sage, 1995.

Index

A

Access, 64

activities. *See* Activity Relationship Diagram; Activity Relationship Matrix

Activity Relationship Diagram
case study: new product development, 143-144
explained, 39-43, 105-107

Activity Relationship Matrix
case study: airline merger, 169-170
case study: logistics service provider, 104-105
case study: new product development, 140-141
closeness rating scale, 36
developing, 35-37
reasons for closeness value, 36
relationship chart, 36

AI (artificial intelligence)
explained, 68, 210-211
methods, 212-211

airline merger (case study), 159-161
decision criteria, developing, 163-168
decision criteria metrics, 166-168
identifying objectives and goals, 163
selecting decision criteria, 164-165
weighting criteria, 165-166
weighting objectives, 163-164

integrated corporate planning approach
Activity Relationship Diagram, 173-174
Activity Relationship Matrix, 169-170
industry benchmarks, 170-173
scope of problem, assessing, 169
specific problem areas to improve, 174-182
objectives, defining, 161-162
problem solving, 192-195
results, evaluating, 195-201
scope of problem, assessing, 182-186
data that supports measurement of objectives, 186-187
defining sphere of control, 183
identifying problem areas, 182-1834
upstream and downstream interactions, 186
sensitivity analysis, 194-199
statistical analysis, 195-201

alternatives, evaluating, 75, 126-127

analysis. *See* data analysis; statistical analysis; what-if analysis

analytical hierarchy process, 223-224

artificial intelligence. *See* AI (artificial intelligence)

FT Press
FINANCIAL TIMES

In an increasingly competitive world, it is quality
of thinking that gives an edge—an idea that opens new
doors, a technique that solves a problem, or an insight
that simply helps make sense of it all.

We work with leading authors in the various arenas
of business and finance to bring cutting-edge thinking
and best-learning practices to a global market.

It is our goal to create world-class print publications
and electronic products that give readers
knowledge and understanding that can then be
applied, whether studying or at work.

To find out more about our business
products, you can visit us at www.ftpress.com.